THE ART

OF

Staying Together

THE ART
OF
Staying
Together

A Couple's Guide to
Intimacy and Respect

Michael S. Broder,
Ph.D.

HYPERION

NEW YORK

Excerpt on pp. 227–30 from M. Broder, *Divorce and Separation,* Chapter 4: "Clinical Applications of Rational-Emotive Therapy," edited by Albert Ellis and Michael Bernard, Plenum Publishing Company, 1985, reprinted by permission.

For information address Hyperion, 114 Fifth Avenue, New York, New York 10011.

Library of Congress Cataloging-in-Publication Data
Broder, Michael S.
The art of staying together : a couple's guide to intimacy and respect / Michael S. Broder.
p. cm.
ISBN 1-56282-883-5
1. Intimacy (Psychology) 2. Man-woman relationships—United States. 3. Marriage—United States. 4. Communication in marriage—United States. I. Title.
HQ801.B858   1993
306.7—dc20   93-31086
CIP

First Edition
10 9 8 7 6 5 4 3 2 1

To Arlene, Joanne, and couples everywhere...

CONTENTS

ACKNOWLEDGMENTS

My heartfelt thanks go out to some of the many people who helped me to make this book a reality:

To Dr. Arlene Goldman, my wife, partner, and colleague whose tremendous wisdom and insight—both personally and professionally—are in some way reflected in every part of this book;

To Judith Riven, my senior editor at Hyperion, for her help and support in shaping the vision of this book and bringing it to fruition;

To Jane Dystel, of Acton and Dystel, my literary agent, for her constant and generous support;

To Oneita Harmon for her tireless devotion to this project, her extraordinary typing, transcribing, and editing skills, and for all of her help in producing the manuscript;

To Ed Claflin who provided me with help in the editing of the manuscript;

To Dr. Albert Ellis, the founder of Rational Emotive Therapy and my mentor, whose ideas continue to influence practically every area of my professional life and are well represented throughout this book;

To my daughter, Joanne, who has taught me more about parenting than anyone else;

To Elaine Smith, Esq., for her legal research; and to Marcia Coward for her early editorial assistance.

I would like to extend my everlasting appreciation to the thousands of clients and couples I have seen in my practice, to the tens of thousands of callers-in to my radio programs, to the members of the many audiences—of every variety—that I have addressed over the years, and to all those I've interviewed, especially for this book, for the lion's share of insight that I hope this book reflects.

Finally, let me express a giant debt of gratitude to all the colleagues, friends, and family members whose support, encouragement, and expertise I've always considered my most valuable resource.

TO THE READER

When I was on tour following the publication of *The Art of Living Single,* one of the questions I was asked most frequently was: "Are you opposed to marriage?" When I answered to the contrary, the question that followed was often: "Then why aren't you now married?" So first I would explain that I am happily coupled. Then I'd explain the giant string that ties together all of the advice I have given in my books, articles, radio programs, lectures, and media appearances. It is this: *There are an infinite number of choices and lifestyles. Taking charge and making your own choices is probably your deepest duty to yourself as a human being.* For example, a choice I made recently was to marry the woman I had been living with for several years. Rarely is as much unhappiness experienced from designing your own life as it is from ignoring your desires and dreams. If you do that, you're living someone else's life rather than your own.

This is as true when you are involved in a love relationship with someone—whether or not you are married—as it is when you are living single. In this book I hope to show you many of the choices that you can arrive at (both alone and with a partner) concerning your relationship. If possible, it would be ideal if you and your partner could read *The Art of Staying Together* and use it as a jumping-off point for deep discussion.

As partners in your choices together, you can shut out the rest of the world, sit down and decide exactly what you want to do with your lives together. If you so choose, you can expand upon your strengths and learn how to deal with your weaknesses so that each of you can win in the relationship.

Not all couples can make their relationship work; but nearly all of us have the capacity to understand our choices and to articulate them clearly to ourselves and to others. In *The Art of Staying Together* you will read stories of couples whose problems may seem quite familiar to you. You will see what choices they needed to make for themselves: If you can identify the options that seem most attractive to you at this time in your life, then you will broaden your own parameters.

Some of what you will read about may not seem at all familiar to you. In some cases it may even offend you. But it is all based on what is really happening today with couples across our culture.

We live in a difficult and confusing time in which the rules are constantly changing. After a fairly stable marriage-based society that existed for centuries, my generation experienced the collapse of that structure. And when that structure fell apart, there was no new one to take its place. Needless to say, many people who are caught in the void are confused, angry, guilty, insecure, and stressed out! The tumultuous sexual revolution and its aftermath changed the lives of singles and couples, and it also posed a challenge to every therapist who was involved in those issues.

The baby-boom generation was raised in a traditional world, with few clues about the upheaval to come. In reports on sexuality in the late forties and early fifties, Kinsey presented some surprising data that showed that there was indeed a great deal of sexual activity in sexually "repressive" times. The Kinsey reports revealed more about people's sexual habits than much of the general public wanted to deal with.

To me, this repressiveness and the hypocrisy of that era is best summed up in the attitudes that were displayed in television shows like *Ozzie and Harriet*. I think these "typical family" sitcoms of the fifties and early sixties could have been some of the more destructive television shows of all times, doing at least as much damage to our collective psyche than the violence and sex on the screen today. *Ozzie and Harriet* and similar shows encouraged expectations of what a family should be to rise to impossible heights. I certainly didn't know any families like the Nelsons. I knew of one that was purported to be like them, in which the kids, like the father, were almost always president of everything they joined, while the mother was the perpetual head of the PTA as well as a staple of church committees. In the end, it turned out that the children eventually had major drug problems, the father committed suicide, and the "loving mother" ran off with another man!

How many of us have tried to emulate this idealized kind of family? And regardless of their modeling, how many have felt inferior because they weren't living up to a totally false set of expectations of what it means to be a couple, and what family life should be? No wonder the walls came tumbling down so readily when the sexual revolution came along.

That revolution was the result of a multitude of factors. The introduction of the birth control pill in 1960 had a major impact on freer sexual behavior. Contemporaneously, my mentor Albert Ellis published a ground-breaking book called *Sex Without Guilt*. The concept of sex solely for pleasure was still considered by many to be scandalous in 1958 when Dr. Ellis's book came out.

The baby-boom generation began to come of age as the birth control pill hit the market. They rebelled against parents who insisted that sex was supposed to be associated with lifelong commitment in marriage. There was an extremely rapid change in attitudes toward sexuality. Almost overnight single women went from being afraid to admit they had sex to being afraid to admit they didn't. I remember once in the seventies when one of my clients, age twenty-five, told me a "terrible deep dark secret"—that she was still a virgin!

With antibiotics easily available, this era was also one of the few times in history when sexually transmitted diseases were rarely fatal or incurable. Until the onset of herpes, people usually could "let it all hang out" without serious medical consequences. Many people did, and not always wisely. While much was learned and experienced, mistakes were made, and many sound and healthy ideas about relationships were exploited. By the mid-seventies, many of the married people I knew, including myself, had broken up with their spouses.

We now have so many choices that we often feel uncomfortable having to make any definite choice at all. Since the prefabricated lifestyles of the past usually don't apply to the present, many couples seem to need more and more help with things they were raised to believe should come as "second nature" to them. I remember when the divorce rate first hit 50 percent in the late 1970s. It was supposed to have been a fluke, but more than a decade later that rate still hovers at over 50 percent. And, of course, that doesn't mean that the couple that stays together will be happy either. Some are afraid to leave their relationships, while others do not even consider the other options for religious, financial, or other reasons.

My view of the high divorce rate is not one of gloom and doom. I believe that the rate reflects a general rise in life expectations. Most people today simply don't accept the idea of staying in an unhappy marriage. In our grandparents' time, many unhappy couples simply moved the two beds apart, put a nightstand in the middle, became roommates, and stayed together. There may have been a lot of fiftieth wedding anniversaries back then, but that doesn't mean they were necessarily happy couples celebrating good marriages. Today we are more likely to make choices that will allow each of us to live happy lives. In the process, there will be divorce as well as the ending of long-term nonmarital relationships.

This book will focus on helping you, the reader, to keep your relationship together and on understanding why it's together, as long as staying together serves you and your partner. If you discover that staying together cannot work for you, I will help you both to know why and then to find a way out.

The Art of Staying Together is divided into three parts. In Part I, we will look at the basic issues that almost all relationships face. In Part II, I will talk about troubled relationships from practically all points of view and what—if anything—can be done to save them. In Part III, we will look at more choices and issues: jealousy, the implications of the monogamous relationship, and the alternatives to it. We then will explore the pros and cons of parenthood. Many couples stay together for the children and for other reasons they often have a difficult time justifying, even to themselves. In Chapter 12, we will explore those options. Next, I will present the implications of leaving a relationship that, for whatever reason, needs to end. In the final chapter, the issue of rechoosing each other will be explored.

Feel free to skip around in the book to those areas that concern you the most about your relationship, or to go to those sections that may help you to gain some insight about a relationship that may have ended, either recently or a long time ago. Perhaps other sections of the book will help you to understand what is going on in the relationship of someone close to you.

Whatever your issues or concerns are, know that you are not alone and that you need not feel stuck. For inside of you lies the wisdom to make the choices that will make your life work, both as an individual and as part of a couple. This book is designed to help you to tap that inner resource.

Good luck!

Michael S. Broder, Ph.D.
Philadelphia, Pennsylvania

THE ART
OF
Staying Together

PASSION AND COMFORT:

The Foundation for Relationships that Work

This is a book about couples, romance, significant others, marriage, spouses, spouse equivalents, friends, mates, lovers, and last, but not least, relationships. It's about living together, fulfilling your own needs, fulfilling each other's needs, and even gaining the wisdom to see when moving on may be in your best interest. If the latter becomes your choice, I will help you to break away.

As a psychologist who's worked with couples for nearly two decades, I've been through the joy and the heartbreak of involvement with many many people. As a man who's been married and divorced and who is now in a happy second marriage, much of what I am going to tell you also comes from my own life experiences.

Professionally and personally, I have always been struck by the difficulty of predicting how any individual will behave in a love relationship. Indeed, when it comes to relationships, I see many people who seem totally inept although they are brilliantly in charge of their lives in every other area. Men and women who normally pride themselves on their personal power sometimes act like rubber-legged beings with no choices in their love relationships.

The difference between these individuals' difficulties with relationships and their success in other aspects of living often comes down to understanding and acting on the many choices at hand. Therefore, let me say that the one recurring theme throughout this book is *choice*. I will show how you and your partner, both unilaterally and together, can make the choices that will lead to satisfaction in this most important area of your lives.

A love relationship, strictly speaking, is only as good as the needs it fulfills in each partner. It has two main elements: *passion* and *comfort*. To the extent that either passion or comfort (or both) are present in your relationship, the involvement you want not only can happen but can continue. Let's take a look at these qualities separately and then see how they interact.

PASSION

Passion is the emotional component of a relationship. Positive passion is generally what brings you together and what makes your partner so special to you. It's experienced as love, attraction, well-being, desire, trust, and joy in being around your partner. Happiness, excitement, and sexual energy are all tied to *positive* passion. The *negative* side of passion, of course, consists of anger, jealousy, fear, and longing.

A relationship based only on passion usually will be marked by extreme highs and lows. Ultimately, it will be stormy or short, or both. A relationship lacking passion altogether will be something akin to a platonic friendship; the most you can probably hope for is to be best friends.

Passion is the spark that draws two people together and that usually provides the ultimate motivation for keeping them together. However, it does not provide the stability that a *long-*

term relationship needs. For that, we must turn to the other element—comfort.

Comfort—warm, easy, natural, accepting—is the day-to-day glue that allows a couple to have an enjoyable and peaceful coexistence. Couples who have stayed together for decades and who describe themselves as happy ultimately point to comfort as the ingredient that sustained their relationship for so long a time.

Comfort is being yourself, to the extent to which you *can* be yourself, in a relationship without being obsessed with pleasing your partner. Comfort is also the extent to which you and your partner share this feeling of ease with one another. Accepting your partner for the person he or she is, being able to deal with conflicts, and having enough things in common (such as life goals) create the kind of psychological environment in which you can nurture and sustain your relationship.

Nonetheless, it is a rare couple that doesn't confront issues that require both partners to change something about themselves in order to resolve these issues. It is also important to note that for comfort to be authentic in a relationship, it needs to be mutually shared. If only one partner is comfortable, then comfort is an illusion. The lack of an acceptable comfort level for either partner usually prompts a breakup or a very difficult time. However, where comfort is mutual, it generally becomes the foundation upon which you can build the strong framework to handle all other issues.

Unfortunately, very few relationships have a satisfactory degree of both passion *and* comfort. So, throughout this book, I will be showing you ways to increase both, if that is your choice.

Since romance is the aura (and the product of passion) that makes a love relationship so special, this book will have much to say about romance. It will, however, avoid romanticizing or encouraging you in any way to create an artificial sense of comfort or well-being. The following are a pragmatist's critical definitions of some important terms to help you to size up your own situation.

Although it's been said that "fools explain it, but wise men never try," my experience has been the opposite. In romantic love's truest form, both passion (the positive kind) and comfort are present. The real litmus test is how you feel about *yourself* when you are either around or thinking about the one you love.

There's a difference between *being* in love (romantically) and actually *loving* someone. If love is reciprocated, the difference between these two conditions doesn't really matter; in other words, it's far easier to go from being in love to loving when your love is returned. You and the person you love derive comfort from loving each other.

But, often, being in love is a fantasy that's unrelated to the reality of whether or not you are loved in return.

Being in love often involves passion *without* comfort and can have little to do with the actual object of your affection, other than your obsession with that person. Perhaps your love is not reciprocated and/or you demand that the other person love you in return. Unrequited love—the stuff songs, plays, books, and movies are made of—often can lead to rage, suspicion, jealousy, and distress of every variety. This kind of one-sided relationship is very common, so common, in fact, that I have devoted an entire chapter to it.

The reality is that nobody can make another person love him or her! Throughout history that truth has been a source of pain (perhaps the most common in the world) for untold numbers of people. If you have suffered this kind of pain, there is good news. To learn to focus your love on an appropriate partner, you first must be willing to deal with the issues that prevent you from loving. In my experience, practically everyone has the capacity to *feel* love for another person. But the ability to feel comfort as well as passion with another person involves more than just feeling love. It means *loving*—and there are many dimensions to that word.

Intimacy is the ability to share your innermost self with another person. Sometimes, but not always, this means opening that part of yourself to which no one else has access. No universal definition exists of what is the right amount of intimacy. All couples ultimately develop their own depth and style of intimacy.

Some couples actually split up because they have shared one or two things too many. (Often they've been able to predict the inevitable result.) I've heard others attribute their long-term success to recognizing how intimate they can be and to understanding what is best left unshared. (In some cases, much is left unsaid.) Yet others claim that they are 100 percent open with each other. (I remain skeptical about this claim!)

The degree to which you are able to establish this crucial intimacy in your relationship can usually be measured by your comfort level as a couple. Indeed, many couples have told me in so many words that real intimacy takes place not in the bedroom but in the living room. I suggest that you think of intimacy in the broadest way possible. Yes, intimacy means sharing many secrets—but it also means sharing many of the common, everyday, and humdrum matters of life. The ability to communicate about the widest range of subjects and concerns is what enhances your growth as a couple.

Commitment has become a buzzword that describes the process by which each person defines his or her desire for a long-term relationship rather than a short-term relationship. In Chapter 2, we will be talking more about how commitment actually happens, but I must warn that both the concept and the word are racked with discrepancies and ambiguities.

For instance, if two people get divorced after one, five, ten, or twenty years of marriage, what does that say about their relationship? That they never really had a commitment? That they *broke* their commitment? I think it's safe to say that they had a commitment to each other even though the marriage ran its course. (And if you are wondering about the commitment in your own past relationships, I will return to this subject later in the book.)

We also hear a great deal these days about people who *"cannot* commit to a relationship." As a psychologist who helps people to achieve the kind of relationship they want, I have often embraced that concept myself when working with those who have difficulties at various stages of involvement.

Lately, however, I've come to see that many who have been perceived as "unable to commit" in one relationship appear to "spontaneously recover" when starting the next. Once the unsuccessful relationship ended, the next relationship with a new partner seemed to trigger few of the issues that had been present in the previous one.

So isn't it fair to ask if the label is valid? Are such a large number of people really "unable to commit"? I've heard precious few people say that a relationship wasn't working because of *their own* inability to make a commitment, yet I've heard scores of people make that diagnosis for present or previous partners.

As a result, I have adopted a workable definition of "commitment." I believe commitment is the agreement that exists between the two partners of a couple to stay together under the rules (spoken or unspoken) that they have established for themselves until one or both partners have a change of mind. Far too few couples acknowledge that reevaluation of their commitment is a constant and ongoing part of every relationship.

RELATIONSHIPS THAT WORK

What, then, makes a relationship work?

Naturally, all relationships are different, but those that work have similarities. When two people decide to stay together in a long-term relationship, what is it that *keeps* them together? In general, they hold on to the two important elements I have already mentioned—passion and comfort.

But in talking to many individuals and couples in therapy, I have discovered a number of much more specific traits and attitudes that characterize the foundation of most workable long-term relationships. A checklist would look like this:

• They recognize that an *issue that affects one person will affect both as a couple.* These couples usually do not consider an issue resolved unless or until they find a win-win solution that favors both.

• They value their relationship *because* it fulfills the needs of each partner.

• They think in terms of each other's *long-range* best interests and exhibit the ability to grow both separately and together.

• They *like, trust, and respect each other.* These feelings transcend their disagreements.

• They *mutually support each other's pursuit of what is important to him or her.* Each partner encourages the other to develop in his or her own unique way. When partners do things and make sacrifices for each other, they don't feel like martyrs. Instead, each knows his or her ability to have and to behave with concern for the other partner is to the advantage of both the couple and of each partner separately.

• They share an acceptable number of *common interests.*

• *They share power.* Neither partner dominates the other. Instead, partners take turns being the balloon and being the string.

• _They do not rely on each other for all of their validation._ They are able to get many of their needs fulfilled outside of their relationship.

• Both partners have a degree of _self-reliance_. They are comfortable with and are able to accept themselves to the same degree they expect acceptance from their mates.

• They have _similar values_ in most important areas and have worked out a way to handle disagreements in others.

• They are _compatible sexually_ to a degree that satisfies each partner.

• They enjoy _playing together_ nonsexually as well.

• They are _interdependent_. They know they can rely on each other and believe that they are stronger acting together than separately.

• They give each other a sufficient amount of _attention and appreciation_.

• They also respect each other's _privacy_ and need at times to "stand on one's own two feet."

• Partners together and separately _take responsibility to give their relationship the time and attention_ it needs and deserves.

In the pages ahead I will tell you not so much what to do but what your choices are. Along the way, I will constantly remind you that you are not alone in your issues. I will also help you to see what others in your shoes have done.

Then, the responsibility to make the choices is yours.

PART ONE

The
Basics

CHAPTER ONE

HOW TO GET PAST THAT FIRST MAJOR BUMP

For practically all of her adult life, Joan had been involved in short-term relationships. Though usually she was the one to initiate the break-up, she had constantly said that what she wanted most was an involvement that would last. When Joan first met someone to whom she was attracted, she had no trouble being "swept off her feet." She would quickly begin to see her new beau as "the one."

After Joan's initial euphoria, her feelings of attraction would begin to wear off. Joan would start finding more and more fault with each partner until either he would react and move on, or she would meet someone else and begin the process all over again.

Joan's favorite saying was: "There are no good men out there who can make a commitment." How many times I have heard this in my practice!

When Joan became involved with Peter she had met her

match. Peter was also a master of short-term relationships. He prided himself on being able to skillfully handle this type of involvement, but said he would gladly change his attitude if "the right woman came along." Although he acknowledged his pattern, he didn't see it as his problem. As he described it: "When things start to get sticky, I feel myself pulling away, realizing that the woman I'm with probably isn't the one."

Peter's method of dealing with relationships had worked fine before he met Joan. But now things were different. Here was a woman Peter cared for who was pulling away before he wanted to end the relationship. At this point, Peter realized he was not quite as much in control as he thought.

At my suggestion, Peter brought Joan into therapy. It took a great deal of effort on their part, but they resolved many issues they had as a couple as well as some that each had separately, which had previously kept each of them from having a long-term involvement.

As of this writing, Joan and Peter are still together. I will explain specifically how they achieved this milestone later in this chapter. But, first, it is important to explore the vast array of obstacles that both men and women who never seem to get past that first major bump generally have in common.

SHORT-TERM VERSUS LONG-TERM RELATIONSHIPS

Short-term relationships can *feel* great. They're the affairs we love to read about in novels and watch in movies. Usually their driving force is passion. When we're in a short-term relationship, we talk about the initial "chemistry." Well, whatever the chemical is that produces the initial attraction and infatuation, it could be the most addictive chemical there is. After all, what on earth could possibly be better than those constant feelings of pleasure and well-being you have when you are infatuated/"in love"?

You will probably agree that little is more nebulous than trying to define "the thing" that makes someone attractive to

you. Think about the people in your life whom you have found attractive. Were you turned on by physical appearance, mannerisms, wit, status, or a common interest? Have you ever had or shared a "special feeling" toward a person? That special feeling is what we call chemistry. You may have experienced it as a rush of energy that makes you want to be around that other person more and more or, at least, to think about that person when he or she is not physically present. Now try to decipher this chemistry. You will find it vague and hard to define. You will realize that you probably cannot easily predict either *when* you will feel this chemistry or *with whom*.

Sometimes, in fact, you will *not* feel "chemistry" when you might have anticipated it. Consider how a prospective partner could have just about every trait you would previously have thought desirable, and still you might not be drawn to that person. Traits alone do not assure that someone will be the least bit attractive to you. Perhaps you've experienced this classic example of the chemistry enigma: You've gone out on a blind date with someone who on paper appeared to fulfill your every need. Yet after spending an evening together, you found that even though there was nothing really wrong between you, you had no desire to see your date again. And you may not even be able to pinpoint why.

The opposite phenomenon is also possible. You may have experienced an initial attraction, crush, fantasy, or infatuation (call it what you wish) that felt great but was directed toward a person with whom you had little in common and little or no positive interaction. You may not have even *liked* this person under any other circumstances. Infatuation does not have to be based on any reality at all. In fact, the person who brings out this rush in you may meet none of your criteria or objectives for a partner.

The greatest fantasy on earth is to have someone in your life forever who will continually trigger that special feeling in you. Notice I said "trigger the feeling in you." Hold on to that thought because later we will discuss what happens when a relationship runs its course. (Often, you are left with the belief that the other person not only left you but also "stole" the

good feeling from you—in other words, you may believe that you may never have those same feelings "triggered" by anyone else ever again.)

The sad truth is that these quick, exciting feelings *do* fade away. Romantic love never lasts forever—and when it fades, you have a more realistic, though probably less glamorous, view of your partner. It's then that you may have to ask yourself whether you like what you see.

After the fantasy side of the initial attraction begins to fade, it may give way to something that is more *real,* more lasting, and more grounded in everyday life than that semihazy state of being in love.

It is rare to find a couple that has turned a short-term involvement into a long-term one without experiencing at least one major crisis that forces a reevaluation of their reasons for being and staying together. What are those reasons? If you are going through such a transitional stage, you might be asking:

• Do I want the relationship to go on to the next level? Have I made a real decision (at least intellectually) about this move?

• Am I willing to take the risks involved? For example, do I feel love for my partner—and, if so, can I be the one to break the ice and say "I love you"?

• Is this person someone with whom I can create an acceptable lifestyle for the two of us?

• Am I truly ready for involvement, or do I merely seek a long-term relationship as a remedy for my loneliness?

• Do I find the other person acceptable *as is?* (Or do I secretly believe that person will change if I "make a commitment"?)

• Do we have enough in common in those areas that matter most, such as lifestyle, social status, religion, sex roles, and values?

• Is this relationship emotionally rewarding?

WHAT IS THE POTENTIAL FOR YOUR RELATIONSHIP?

There was a very popular book written several years ago by Laurence F. Peter called *The Peter Principle*. It talked about how common it is for people to rise to a level of incompetence in work situations. The book gave many good examples of superb workers being incompetent as supervisors, of good supervisors failing once they became managers, and of good managers coming undone when promoted to top executive roles. Indeed, we live in a society that values advancement.

So what does this have to do with your involvement? The Peter Principle and its variations apply even more aptly to relationships. Think about how many of these examples have happened to you:

- You have a platonic friendship with a member of the opposite sex that fails when the two of you try to date or become sexual.
- A great dating relationship falls apart when either one of you makes the slightest gesture toward exclusivity.
- A short-term passionate relationship falls apart when someone begins to talk long-term.
- A long-distance relationship dissolves when either discussions about or attempts at moving closer take place, or after you actually move in together.
- Living together seems to work fine, so you both consider the next logical step—marriage—and the entire relationship is jeopardized.
- A married couple does extremely well for as long as five or ten years, but the marriage no longer seems to work when a baby enters the scene.

Do you get the idea? A love relationship is an excellent example of the adage "A convoy is as fast as its slowest ship." No matter what the process, ultimately the one who wants less involvement usually sets the limits within which the relationship will operate.

Another important premise that I strongly believe and want you to consider is that *relationships that end don't fail, they merely run their course.* Have you ever had a blind date with someone with whom you were so mismatched that you mutually agreed to end the evening before it ever really started? We can certainly say that that relationship ran its course rather quickly; or perhaps it was a three- or four-month relationship that never went any further; or a ten-, or twenty-, or forty-year marriage that ended in divorce. Regardless of the reason for the breakup, remember our definition of commitment: an agreement made between two people until one of them has a change of mind. And what happens when the commitment ends—when one person does change his or her mind? In all likelihood it is a signal that the relationship has run its course.

But let's assume that the two of you are compatible in the general areas of passion and comfort. Take a moment to sit back and determine whether you are reasonably satisfied with your partner. What drew you to each other in the first place? And what's likely to *keep* you together in the long term? Let's consider some factors.

PHYSICAL ATTRACTIVENESS

In the final analysis, physical attractiveness could be the most overrated feature one looks for, particularly in a long-term relationship. Think about some of the people you've known throughout your life, who have actually become more physically attractive in your eyes as you came to know them better. On the other hand, see if you can recall a red-hot romantic fling with someone you once thought to be a perfect "10," only to have found that there was little "steak beneath the sizzle." Ironically, that initial physical attraction that you rated a "10" may have dropped to "3" or "4" the more you got to know the person.

Certainly, some physical characteristics (height, weight, build, and facial features) are important to you, but be careful that you don't make the classic mistake of trying to compare your partner to some media image.

AGE

This is another factor on which many people get hung up. Most believe that the man should be older than the woman, but on a practical level does this make sense? Biologically speaking, the woman should be six to ten years older, since men tend to live shorter lives than women. (Note the predominance in retirement communities of white-haired widows over so few widowers.) Fortunately, more and more older women–younger men relationships are beginning to surface. Perhaps someday they will balance out this lopsided, long-standing trend. Extreme age differences in couples are another matter, but your choice here prevails, and I refer you to the traits below that can be consequences of age differences.

INTELLIGENCE

Now we're getting to the stuff of which long-term relationships are made—or broken. Very few relationships survive unless both people have a fairly compatible range of intelligence. Intellectual compatibility, however, is not necessarily determined by educational level or IQ. Instead, I would say that the most important factor is whether you and your partner feel as if you can understand each other intellectually and share some of the same intellectual interests. Think of a person with whom at one time or another you have felt intimidated, uncomfortable, or even ignorant in normal conversation. Compare this with someone else with whom you have had the opposite experience. You may have concluded that the first individual had no grasp or understanding about those things you enjoy discussing. Such a person is one from whom drifting apart is likely.

PSYCHOLOGICAL CHARACTERISTICS

Under this category, think about what you consider a satisfactory degree of self-esteem, maturity, temperament, familiarity, and patience. Think about people in your past whose temperament allowed you to relax together easily. Think about other psychological characteristics that are significant to you as well. These are extremely important aspects to consider when determining ultimate compatibility.

WHO THEY ARE IN THE WORLD

In this area, of course, only you can fill in the blanks. Income, professional and occupational status, lifestyle, and props all enter into this one. I only caution you to be aware of a tendency to want everything.

WHO THEY ARE WITH YOU

Up until now, I've asked you to use your head. Now it's time to let your heart take over. How do you feel with this person? How do you relate sexually? Can you be intimate on other levels? Do you share enough in common to make your time together interesting and enjoyable? Think about all of the people who at one time or another have passed this last and most important hurdle in your life, whether the relationship turned out to be a long-term one or not. What do those relationships that involve intimate sharing have in common? Or, to put it another way—what turns you on? Try to look within yourself to get as much information as you can about the private side of you. The intimacy that you can share is probably the most important factor when determining—in your heart of hearts— whether you want a relationship to continue.

Assuming that you are looking for long-term involvement, consider the values that always must be present to an acceptable degree for a relationship to be sustained. By "values" I mean more than agreeing on what is good or bad. Your shared values will influence many aspects of your long-term relationship, including . . .

- How conflicts and disputes will be settled.
- How much sharing of emotions and emotional honesty take place within the relationship.
- How money will be handled.
- Sexual compatibility.
- Ideas about family life.
- Desires to bear and raise children.
- Work habits of each partner.
- Standard of living with which each is comfortable.
- Geographic location, type of community and housing.
- Selection of friends.
- The role of in-laws and other important people in your partner's life.
- Feelings about personal growth and directions where you can grow together and apart.
- Future goals of each partner and of the couple.
- Amount of time spent together.
- How time together is spent.
- How much each of you can tolerate and encourage your partner's activities with people outside of the relationship.
- How much time can be spent apart by each partner.
- Religious practices.
- Raising of children when differences in religious or educational practices exist.

> ## HAS THIS EVEN GOT A CHANCE?

When "How to Fall in Love Again with the Same Person" was the topic of my radio program, one caller jokingly remarked, "I have no problem falling in love with the same person. I do it over and over and over again. The only two problems are they always come in a different body and they never reciprocate." Of course that became a topic for another show. And the response to *that* show proved that this is an excruciatingly common problem.

I am sure that like most of us, you have had your share of "usual suspects," those personalities with whom you cannot win. You know who they are. Long-term involvement with them, at least for you, is impossible. Perhaps a short-term relationship is all the potential that may be present. These may be people who want to leave once the conquest is made. On the other hand, you may have experienced a relationship with someone who isn't about to leave, but nonetheless just doesn't seem to be a long-term partner for you. Maybe there are just too many issues between the two of you and not enough motivation to resolve them.

As long as you don't delude yourself into believing that such a person will change, it's perfectly okay to have some involvement with this kind of person. But that's a tall order. Often we do believe a partner will change, simply because we want them to. For this reason there are a number of romantic situations that it would probably be best to avoid.

REBOUND RELATIONSHIPS

People involved in rebound relationships are usually not psychologically ready to let a new person in. Perhaps they're in so much pain that they don't really know who you are. Although the passion and comfort levels can quickly become remarkably high, rebounders often have not worked through the pain they still feel for their ex-mates. Once they do, there is a good chance that there won't be a basis for the two of you to stay involved. Be wary of anyone who has left a marriage or another intense relationship within the last year. In all likelihood, someone who has recently ended such a relationship is still carrying a great deal of pain, so they can't see you clearly as a person until they've become emotionally free of that last relationship.

PREBOUND RELATIONSHIPS

I've seen so much of this recently in my practice that I've coined a special term for it. Prebound relationships generally apply to involvement with people who are seeking new partners *while still* married or very much involved with their last relationship. They are, quite honestly, looking for new partners to provide psychological anesthesia and safety nets for the time when the existing relationship breaks up. Warning: Prebound relationships are generally of a one-sided nature. More often than not, however, both rebounders and prebounders are acting out of intense pain—not malice. Thus, they are rarely aware of their motives. They will be discussed more thoroughly in Chapter 7.

ABUSERS

These potential partners come in all varieties. They can be physically or emotionally abusive to you, or they can be abusing themselves by excessive use of drugs or alcohol. If you are involved with an abuser who denies the problem and does not seek help, be assured that the behavior will change only for the worst. This is true until the abusive pattern is acknowledged by him or her. Abusers rarely make permanent changes in themselves merely because they were asked, persuaded, or forced to do so by partners. Unless one wants help to change, permanent change won't happen. How long you want to hang in there is your choice. You could have a long wait. The problems these people present, according to the stage of involvement, will be discussed in different chapters throughout the book.

BOTTOMLESS PITS

Individuals who do a great deal of taking but give little in return. Although one could be with you for the duration, rest assured that you are seen more as a parent than as an equal partner. Endless demands will be put on you, sometimes early in the relationship, sometimes later. When you *stop* giving, the bottomless pit moves on to the next relationship. The earlier in the relationship that you do stop giving in to extreme demands, the better off you will be. It's highly unlikely that this person will stop making demands on you; therefore, it's very important to make choices for yourself, even if that means ending the relationship completely.

AMBIVALENCE

When I wrote *The Art of Living Single,* I interviewed many people who did not like the single lifestyle. Some went so far as to say that life would not be worth living unless they could enter into a long-term relationship. But even those with the most extreme dislike for the single lifestyle admitted that they would have a difficult time giving up two things. The first is the *freedom* that characterizes being unattached. The second is the *fantasy* of finding that "perfect" partner.

Indeed, I have met very few people who could not have a long-term relationship if only they worked on issues that make them resist involvement. Perhaps the issue to address first is what may be your own ambivalence about being involved.

Ambivalence is an inability to decide. Some people are ambivalent in certain areas of their lives. Others find that ambivalence touches every aspect of their being. If you are a highly ambivalent person, you have probably seen your ambivalence cause you unending pain in one way or another. In fact, ambivalence can actually ruin your life. That's right! Even if theoretically you had everything going for you but you were ambivalent about making life decisions, no matter what your assets, no matter what you chose to do, you would probably dwell on the belief that you "should" be doing something else. That's ambivalence in a nutshell. No matter what choices you have made for yourself, ambivalence can ruin your perception of it all.

Of course, we all have a certain degree of ambivalence. Since life is such an extremely complicated process, things usually get more and more complex as we go along. A certain amount of ambivalence is normal and expected. In fact, a small amount of ambivalence might even serve to protect you from being thoughtless about certain decisions. The greatest problem with ambivalence, however, is that it allows you to operate under an often *unspoken* myth. That myth is that there is one absolutely right answer for every question (or deliberation), and that it is possible somehow to find total security and certainty.

Ambivalent people often mistakenly believe that by being indecisive and by holding out long enough, they will eventually arrive at that one right answer. Or that the answer will simply but magically come to them. The myth is perpetuated by the belief that you can't, or shouldn't, make mistakes or have any regrets whatsoever about decisions made. Obviously, all of these beliefs act to discourage you from taking the risks that characterize change and all important decisions.

Another way of looking at ambivalence is as a demand for something that really doesn't exist: the guarantee of certainty. This demand is fueled by the fear of making a mistake. When it comes to taking a relationship to the next step, perhaps you demonstrate an ambivalence that is triggered by any of a whole array of *fears*.

Consider the following checklist of those possible fears. Each of them can keep you out of that long-term relationship indefinitely, no matter how appropriate and desirable your potential partner may be. Look carefully at this list, and be honest. Do you recognize any of these fears in yourself?

• If this relationship continues, I'll just be serving as a missing link in my *partner's* life.

• While my partner's needs will be fulfilled, mine won't. I will never get in return the caring that I will be expected to give my partner.

• Being involved will be a constant struggle, making it impossible to balance my needs between independence and closeness.

• I fear *self-disclosure*. The more I reveal of myself, the more likely it is that I will be rejected.

• If things get too intimate and intense, I will lose the ability to direct my own life.

• I will become too attached. When my partner decides to leave me, it will be too painful and I won't be able to handle it emotionally.

• I will be controlled and manipulated.

• I will become lost in the struggle between my desire and my vulnerability.

• If I show any of my power, my partner will perceive me as being too competitive and threatening.

• I will surely be the victim of my partner's infidelity.

• By getting too involved with my partner, I will be subjected to his macho behavior or her feminism.

• My partner will become overly dependent on me.

• I will lose my freedom, privacy, or other aspects of the single lifestyle that I enjoy, and I will then become much more unhappy than I could be on my own.

• I will have to give up time with single friends, hobbies, and other fun that I don't share with my partner.

• Although my partner and I have a good relationship now, it will change for the worse if the relationship is upgraded.

• Getting more involved at this time will overburden me financially.

• I will become burdened with my partner's children and other family. My partner will resist and resent obligations toward my children and family.

• The minute I make a commitment to my partner to proceed toward a long-term relationship, the real "Mr. (or Ms.) Right" will come along. I will then miss the opportunity for which I've waited all my life—to be with that perfect person, the one who will make me feel wonderful all the time.

• My partner will turn out to be an entirely different person once the knot is tied; and my real fear is that our relationship will turn into a remake of my parents' marriage, a situation in which I could never imagine happiness.

Ambivalence often represents a major split between the head and the heart. One of the most frequently repeated phrases in my office is, "I know it intellectually but . . ." The driving force behind that statement is almost always ambivalence.

Earlier in this chapter I outlined some important criteria that you would be wise to consider in assessing your decision for involvement. I hope that list helped you to see whether your ambivalence is preventing you from making an unwise decision that could be disastrous, or whether ambivalence is behind your resistance to the next natural and workable phase of your relationship.

For now, I will assume that you have decided, at least intellectually, that you would like to see your present relationship progress to the next stage, but that your anxieties concerning long-term involvement are getting in the way. To resolve your ambivalence, think of ambivalence as a habitual way of thinking. Habits are learned. They can therefore be unlearned. Adopting new attitudes is the way to undo old ones.

The following alternative attitudes will help to make possible the involvement you want. They will go a long way toward resolving your ambivalence and opening the door to new opportunity, growth, and choice.

• *Committing yourself to a long-term relationship is never without risk.* Like any important decision, it must be made on the basis of incomplete data. Only you can assess the worst possible consequences of a decision that you will ultimately regret. Neither I nor anyone else can tell you what to do. But I do encourage you to decide something *consciously*. Each time you act, you chip away a bit more at that quite destructive ambivalence. Eventually, you will see that the worst thing for you is not to act at all.

• Think of ambivalence as a form of perfectionism. Is there anyone on earth toward whom you would not have *some* ambivalence? Do you think that there is such a thing as a relationship made in heaven? (I've seen many of them that were made in the other place, but never one made there.) Perfectionism is one of the most common obstacles people ultimately put forth to sabotage otherwise workable relationships. If you are looking for the perfect person, your search will be endless. I call that search the "Frankenstein" syndrome. In his quest to create the perfect person, Dr. Frankenstein gathered into a new body the outstanding physical parts of several people. We all know the result.

If you are comparing your real flesh and blood partner to an extremely appealing yet nonexistent fantasy—a perfect mate—I can tell you right now that your partner will never measure up. You will doubtlessly defeat yourself if you are creating a composite of the personality and physical and material characteristics of many different people you have known. To see what I mean, turn the question around. Can you truthfully state that your partner is getting as flawless a mate as you are demanding?

• *There is no perfect relationship.* Don't be fooled by appearances, and don't compare your relationship to someone else's. I've seen too many individuals and couples do this, and it is almost never a fair comparison. Others will tell you only what they want you to know. Most of us have heard entirely different versions of friends' relationships *after* they broke up from what we heard while the couple was together and appearing to be perfectly suited to one another.

Being imperfect is one of the very few things we all have in common, and being human is—by definition—being imperfect. We can only coexist happily to the extent that we accept this in each other. But if you choose otherwise, you'll only have to tolerate imperfection in *yourself.* So to the extent that you're willing to give up the search for perfection, your life will turn around dramatically.

• *Believing that you're not worthy of the kind of long-term involvement you want may be just another way that you put yourself down.* However, you take a great burden off yourself if you can trust your partner to decide—without your "coaching"— whether you're worthy. If you question your partner's worth or credibility as his or her feelings for you get stronger, you are only putting yourself down. Anytime you discount, devalue, or discredit your partner's opinion of you, you're merely finding a way to think less of yourself.

• *When your relationship is moving toward the next phase, it is perfectly normal for the initial chemistry to lessen.* Don't take this as a "sure sign" that it's time to move on. View this period as part of the emotional hazing that every long-term relationship goes through.

• *Keep believing in yourself.* We've all made poor decisions, and hindsight is 20/20, but don't let that diminish your sense of self-worth, either. If we had known then what we know now, we would all do things differently. But that's not an option, so stop pretending it is.

Perhaps you've suffered untold pain when a previous relationship ended, and you fear that by getting too involved it will happen again. No matter how bad that experience was, you lived through it. Having seen many people through ended relationships, I have observed that getting over a breakup usually becomes *easier* to handle—not harder—the second, third, and fourth time, and so on, though many refuse to believe that's possible. It can be quite hard to let yourself get involved, unless you know that, difficult as it will be, *you will survive a breakup.* If you have just emerged from an ended relationship that you have not yet overcome emotionally, you may be on the rebound. If that's the case, it's possible that you are not yet ready for either short- or long-term involvement right now.

• *Talking about your ambivalence with your partner could be your first major issue.* It is this type of sharing that enhances intimacy. Your partner would be a rare person if he or she (whether admittedly or not) was not also experiencing some ambivalence. Discuss your feelings openly and nonjudgmentally. When you get past this one together and wind up accepting yourselves and each other in the process, you may feel closer than you ever could have imagined.

If you found my earlier statement that ambivalence can ruin your life a little strong, you may be taking comfort in ambivalence. Like many people, you may actually take comfort in feeling that relationships are perpetually "up in the air" or in doubt. When you really don't like things as they are but perceive change as too scary to undertake, you may be attracted to a "comfortable state of discomfort." Deciding to end the relationship—or deciding to make a long-term commitment—might upset the fragile balance. My stand on ambivalence is unambivalent. *To the extent that it exceeds prudent caution, ambivalence will hold you back not only in relationships but in every area of your life.*

When all else fails, lighten up! Chances are you are taking yourself way too seriously. Don't turn the hassle of uncertainty into a horror.

GOING FROM SHORT-TERM TO LONG-TERM

As you can see, when making this crucial transition toward a long-term relationship, many decisions need to be made as well as realities taken into consideration. Some decisions happen effortlessly, perhaps without conscious thought, while others may require tremendous unilateral or joint effort. If you and your partner can pull this off, you will rarely regret the effort.

The following are some additional points to consider in making that transition from a short-term to a long-term relationship.

• Take as much time to get to know your partner as you need. Long-term relationships cannot be rushed. Three months to a year is the average time needed to *begin* the transition. That test of time is really the only reliable way to distinguish love from infatuation.

• The attraction and initial chemistry that got the relationship started are not the same forces that will make it continue. Your ability to resolve issues as a couple is a much more important factor in determining whether you will stay together.

• Remember that bottom-line question you should ask yourself about a potential long-term partner: Does this person, without alterations, meet at least the minimum criteria I have set for my partner? If yes, then you certainly have something to work with. If no—or yes only with alterations—then, ultimately, it probably won't work.

• While working together to build the comfort level each of you needs to make the transition from short-term to long-term, the trick is to hold on to an acceptable amount of passion.

• Moving from a short-term to a long-term relationship is not determined by time. A short-term relationship is one that doesn't survive major issues. (Usually the first big one does it.) By that definition, I have known short-term relationships that have lasted as long as ten years.

• A relationship is not necessarily a cure for loneliness. Many people have told me that some of their loneliest times have been when they were very much involved.

• Try this exercise. Project five years into the future. This exercise is similar to aging a picture. Can you see yourselves together then? Pay attention to what you can visualize as your level of passion and comfort.

• If someone in a short-term relationship breaks up with you uncaringly, consider that you have been done a favor. Don't think of yourself as a victim. You are now free to pursue the rest of your life rather than devoting any more of it to a relationship that was probably an illusion. The fact that someone has had only short-term relationships in the past doesn't indicate an inability to get involved. It could mean only that they have thus far been unable to make that transition. But believe someone who tells you that he or she doesn't want further or deeper involvement with you.

• Sex may never be as good as it was the first time, and your passion may never be as strong as it was during the initial attraction. In addition, as real life sets in, it's even appropriate to expect some boredom. Those who continually seek short-term relationships are unwilling or incapable of accepting these ideas.

• In a long-term relationship, anger is not a reason to think that the relationship is over. It is important for each of you to know that your partner will be there when the anger subsides. An excellent sign that a relationship is working is when neither party flees literally or psychologically during tense times.

Now let's go back to Joan and Peter. As I said earlier, Peter came to see me in therapy with issues common to those who have difficulty turning short-term relationships into long-term ones. Peter was typical because so many like him come into therapy when a relationship that they value ends by the other person's choice.

Peter talked about Joan as the one woman he felt he could have married. Yes, Peter pursued her and they had another go-around. Since Peter was taking this relationship so much more seriously than any other he had had previously, I suggested that he bring Joan in for some joint sessions. At first Peter resisted this idea, but he finally arranged joint sessions when he saw the relationship once again veering toward an end.

As I pointed out at the beginning of the chapter, Peter and Joan had a tremendous amount in common regarding their previous relationships. For example, they each had a very low tolerance for someone else's anger. It became clear to each of them how anger typically would cause them to flee. Thus when conflicts arose, each of them had previously found it to be easier to replace the partner than to deal with the conflict. Then, too, each of them was quite attractive and skilled at meeting other people to date.

Although they were angry at their ex-partners, the anger dissipated fairly quickly when they met someone new. That invigorating chemistry that comes with meeting a new person helped them to replace anger with expectation—and they were off again on a new short-term relationship.

Each knew intellectually that what they wanted was a long-term relationship (Peter was thirty-two and Joan twenty-nine), but unconsciously neither of them believed that a long-term relationship offered anything as special as that rush of initial chemistry each had experienced so many times. By learning to accept each other's occasional anger and learning that an issue can be worked through mutually, both were able to give up the type of short-term relationships they had previously mastered for one that became long-term. By exploring the possibilities with each other—instead of looking outside their relationship—they began to discover ways in which a long-term relationship could be so much more fulfilling.

Today, Joan and Peter are working toward mastering a long-term relationship. And as they echoed during their last session: "If we can do it, there's hope for everyone."

CHAPTER TWO

SETTING THE "RULES"

Every relationship has its rules. These rules define what can and cannot take place between you and your partner, and define what constitutes normality (which is why they're sometimes referred to as norms). When you "break" those rules, you and your partner are likely to come into conflict either with yourselves or with each other. Some rules may be consciously, delicately, and/or meticulously determined. Others may be based on "ideals," or they might be "rules" that you learned from your parents. The latter types are often determined unconsciously. And when you're obeying unconscious rules, you may believe that you have no choice—that there's only one way you "can" or "should" behave when you're in a relationship.

Janet and Robert were in their early forties when they came into counseling. They had been married twenty-one years and had three children, ages nineteen, seventeen, and fourteen.

Janet was a housewife; but since the birth of her first child, she had done part-time work to earn some extra (but non-essential) money. Robert was an insurance agent who took a great deal of pride in the fact that he worked hard and provided well for his family.

When their youngest child was about to enter high school, Janet announced that she wanted to take advantage of the additional free time to go back to school and start a career as an elementary school teacher. Though she had talked about this ambition many times during their marriage, Robert had never really taken her seriously. When Robert finally realized that Janet meant business, the couple went into crisis!

"It's as if I have no say in this matter whatsoever. I've seen to it that my family has had everything that they've needed for twenty-one years. Why do you want to change things now?" Robert demanded of Janet in my office.

Janet had seen several of her friends begin careers. She had become an avid reader of self-help books and was beginning to become particularly interested in the contemporary feminist point of view. She was fully prepared to argue with Robert's line of reasoning.

"Throughout our whole marriage we've been playing by your rules," she told Robert. "We've been clones of our parents. I can't say that's all been wrong. But I have to look ahead to the rest of my life." "I don't feel a sense of purpose anymore," she said to Robert at one point. "How am I going to feel when the children don't need me anymore? I'm afraid of what will happen when they leave."

To Robert these doubts of hers came "out of the blue." And they threatened him. If she wasn't satisfied with their life as it was, what did she really want? Where would her "new demands" end?

In taking a look at this common crisis a few things were apparent. Robert's issues were:

• Anger at Janet for not consulting him about her decision. Instead she had already made her decision when she informed him. He felt as though he had no say in what she did.

• Feelings of inadequacy. He believed that Janet was unappreciative of his efforts to be a breadwinner and that she was dissatisfied with what he provided for her. He saw her new career as giving her something that she wasn't getting from him.

• His fear that Janet would become "too independent" and would no longer need or want the marriage to continue.

• Security and stability. He was afraid that Janet would become so absorbed in her studies and in her new career that she would neglect her duties as a parent and a wife.

Janet's issues were:

• Boredom with her present life (since being a mother was no longer as demanding as it used to be); anger at Robert for not supporting her in pursuing her dream and at Robert's insensitivity to her needs.

• Depression. There was little that she saw in her future to arouse her enthusiasm. Only the thought of pursuing her education and starting a new career seemed to make her feel better.

• A general sense of unhappiness as she realized that displeasing Robert could throw the marriage into complete turmoil. It was even conceivable that they would separate.

After much discussion, it became clear to all of us that one of two things would be happening in the very near future. Either some long-standing rules of this marriage would have to be changed or the marriage would not continue.

THREE TYPES OF RULES COUPLES LIVE BY

We all have rules in our relationships—and Robert and Janet were no exception. Generally the rules fit into three different categories: rules that are *spoken*, rules that are *unspoken*, and those that are *automatic*.

SPOKEN RULES

These are generally the easiest to deal with. Couples may not agree to the same set of "spoken" rules, but at least they are clear about what those rules are. For example, Janet and Robert had spoken rules that included the following: (1) Robert would be the breadwinner and Janet would stay at home caring for the children; (2) They would jointly decide where they lived and how they spent their spare time; (3) Decisions about vacations and similar family functions would be subject to mutual agreement. Indeed, Robert and Janet were very compatible in most areas. Matters such as child-rearing, religion, and finances were rarely problems for the two of them. When such issues arose, they were usually able to resolve them easily.

UNSPOKEN RULES

The second category are those rules that are generally not talked about, even though each partner knows very clearly where he or she stands. In this category are a number of things that usually are not discussed with your partner. It took a while for Janet to share the fact that her lifestyle was not nearly as fulfilling to her as Robert thought it was. One of the unspoken rules of their relationship was that Janet would not talk to Robert about feeling depressed or frustrated. She "broke" this rule in my office when she talked about feeling unfulfilled. Not surprisingly, Robert said, "I never knew you felt that way!"

No wonder. It was an unspoken rule of their marriage that when she "felt that way," she would not talk to him about it. To hear about those feelings surprised him, because it was part of their "pact" with each other that she would keep them hidden. Having a therapist in the room made it far easier to verbalize something that was difficult for Janet to say to Robert alone. Her unspoken rule had been: "It's all right to want a career, to feel limited as a housewife and mother—as long as your husband doesn't find out you feel unfulfilled."

Robert, on the other hand, had a different unspoken rule:

If Janet were away from the house, if she went to school and started her career, then he assumed she would end up being unfaithful.

The question was: Why did Robert make this assumption? He confided to me that he had had a few one-time trysts during his business trips. He understandably felt awkward about sharing this information with Janet, since he feared she would be jealous, unhappy, and angry. One of his unspoken rules was: "It's no big deal if I stray every once in a while as long as Janet doesn't find out about it; but if she does, it's totally unacceptable."

AUTOMATIC RULES

These are often the most difficult rules to deal with because they are adopted unconsciously by one or both partners. Many couples become clones of their own families of origin. Essentially, Robert had been assigned the primary responsibility for determining his family's lifestyle. Janet's role was to care for the home and to provide unqualified moral support for her husband and the children. These were the "rules," but neither Robert nor Janet knew that they had unconsciously accepted this set of rules when they married each other.

Both of them came from traditional families, so their whole image of how a marriage was set up and what a family was like came from *their* growing-up experiences. So the pattern of their lifestyle "just happened" when they were married. In fact, they never even discussed the possibility of waiting to have children so Janet could get an education and start her career before childbearing. Before they could begin to negotiate about unconscious rules, they had to recognize what those rules were—and discover that they didn't *have* to accept them. Though they had unconsciously (or automatically) accepted the traditional family arrangement up to this point, that didn't mean the pattern had to continue. Together, they *could* change the family to a new and different "norm."

Before we go any further, think for a moment about what some of your rules may be. See if you can identify some from each category. Try not to judge, but instead just recognize that these are the guidelines that you will be most likely to follow as you live your life and enter into relationships. The good news is that once you recognize them, you're always free to accept, reject, challenge, and change these rules. But before you take that next step, you need to recognize those rules for what they are.

If you'd like to attempt an exercise that could open up some choices for you, try this: Imagine that for one beautiful moment you could be free of all your rules—spoken, unspoken, and automatic. (Undoubtedly there are some rules that you don't want to give up. And why should you? That's your choice too.) Now, if you are totally free of obligatory rules, how will you change your life? It's a rare person who wouldn't change something.

Maybe your changes would be drastic. Maybe they would be minor. What's important is that you let yourself dream from time to time about how your life would change if you could be truly liberated. Then put back into place only the rules you choose. How does this feel?

If you and your partner try this together, discuss the experience that each of you had. Then discuss how you can incorporate some of this insight into your relationship.

> ## THINGS TO KEEP IN MIND WHEN SETTING THE RULES FOR YOUR RELATIONSHIP

Like many couples who face crisis, Janet and Robert wanted to be told specifically what was "right" and what was "wrong," and they wanted the "correct" solution to their problem. Getting each of them to accept their individual roles in this joint determination was the most difficult part of coming to a resolution.

While rules are certainly not universal, you might want to consider these thoughts when coming up with your own guidelines.

• A couple is really an artificial entity. What is most important is that the needs of the individuals—that is, the needs of both you *and* your partner—are addressed. Rules that consistently favor one partner over the other ultimately will not work for either of you.

• Avoid looking at yourself as having "sold out" when you concede to something that's important to your partner. Remember, it is to *your* advantage to please your partner, as it will greatly increase the probability of your partner reciprocating.

• Practically any relationship can look like a good one if there's no stress on it. So no matter what you agree on, expect that there will be some conflict—particularly with respect to stickier issues. Your rules will require a great deal of fine-tuning. And they're likely to change during the course of your relationship—as they did for Janet and Robert. So it's important to be open to changing the rules as your individual and joint needs go through changes. Those who expect one set of "perfect rules" to last a lifetime can anticipate almost perpetual disappointment!

• The earlier you establish rules in a relationship, the better. I once knew a man who always went on a hunting trip with his friends during the week between Christmas and New Year's. When he became involved with a new girlfriend, he mentioned this annual trip quite often while they were getting to know each other. She was not at all surprised when he took this usual week-long trip; it never became a problem for them. (In a previous relationship he had waited until just two weeks before the trip to mention his plans, and the abrupt announcement had wrecked havoc.) If you are someone who has always had opposite-sex confidants, that is usually an item that's much more easily accepted at the beginning of your involvement than if it pops up later on.

• It's never too late to begin discussing issues that have made you unhappy all along, as well as new issues in the relationship. Part of maturity is realizing that human beings do change, and relationships have to make allowances for these changes. In relationships that work over the long term, each partner can accept change not only in themselves but also in the other person.

• Set up a customary way to deal with disputes. It's important to be able to discuss crucial issues at times when you're getting along well. This is, in a sense, a psychological prenuptial agreement—that you will continue to talk about issues and try to come to an understanding, even though these issues may make you angry at times. If you try to work out a problem in the heat of anger, or if you both retreat into silent resentment, it's unlikely the problem will be resolved. Thus, both of you will do much better if you have some agreed-upon ways in which you can initiate these crucial discussions.

• Successful couples often have to live with certain rules that one person doesn't particularly like but that he or she accepts out of regard for the other person. I've never seen a relationship where both people agreed with each other on every point. If you're unwilling to live with at least some traits that you don't like in the other person, chances are that you will never really have a long-term relationship. Remember that some of your rules will conflict with your partner's. In establishing those rules, it may be difficult to arrive at mutual consent until you have patiently considered many alternatives.

• While flexibility is key, in reality both you and your partner are likely to remain inflexible about certain issues. There are really three levels of flexibility.

1. You may have some chosen values that you do *not* consider negotiable, such as career decisions, religion, and nonacceptance of extramarital affairs (whether yours or your partner's).
2. You may feel strongly about other value issues, but at the same time you can see where it is to your advantage to be open to your partner's views. For example, you might be open to altering your views about the number of children you're going to have; or the ways you and your partner express yourselves to each other sexually; or the ways you deal with each other's parents; or how you handle finances together.

3. Finally, there are those things that you may not care about at all that may have much more meaning to your partner. In these instances you can "give in" to your partner or find an easy alternative. For example, one man complained how annoyed he was that his wife did not like to share the Sunday paper until she was all done with it. Obviously, it was important to her to read the paper clear through from beginning to end. To settle the issue, they wound up getting two Sunday papers—a small price to pay to end a small but recurring conflict.

Robert and Janet were able to resolve their crisis largely by looking at the spoken and unspoken rules by which they were living. They also began to recognize some of the unconscious rules that they had lived by ever since they were married— and, having recognized them, they were able to discuss them. Some rules they chose to keep, others they chose to change. In some instances it took agreement between them, while in others each partner had to make a separate decision.

In the end, Janet went ahead with Robert's blessings and completed her degree. She now has a job teaching in elementary school and has begun work on her master's degree. But the resolution involved a definite amount of restructuring of their relationship. When I first met them, Robert was much happier than Janet with the unconscious rules that they had brought to their marriage from their families of origin. In order to see that Janet's career move was not the threat he imagined it to be, Robert had to reexamine his own rules and he also had to accommodate Janet.

Could he see the dividends? For starters, he was living with a happier woman. In addition, the increased income would make it much easier to send their children to college. More income also meant that other luxuries were now within their reach.

Robert also had to revise his image of himself as someone who had it entirely in his power to "make Janet happy." Once he realized that, he could acknowledge that Janet's decision did not imply that he was inadequate in performing his role as her husband. Robert discovered that he was capable of hearing about her unhappiness without trying to "fix it" himself. Janet could verbalize more easily when she didn't have to "justify" herself to him. And this was important because Janet had felt guilty about wanting to define herself outside of the marriage—beyond her role as wife and mother.

Unconsciously, it turned out, Robert had always thought that children would be neglected if their mother wasn't available to them all the time. So the "unconscious rule" had to come to the surface, and the two of them had to work out the issue of "neglecting the kids." Each partner realized that they would have to negotiate their time with the children and with each other more consciously than they had in the past.

In therapy Robert did not share with Janet the fact that he had been unfaithful at times. However, he did share with her his fears that *she* might be unfaithful once she entered the working world. This issue remained unresolved between them, but their improved communication gave them a way of dealing with some of the anxiety it aroused.

Janet was able to understand Robert's fears as well. Coming from a traditional family, he didn't know how a family could function with a wife who had her own career. Since Janet also came from a traditional family, her desire to pursue professional objectives flew in the face of unconscious rules that she also accepted. And it made it hard for her to point to any specific reason or rationale for her choice (which, of course, Robert wanted to hear). Janet couldn't point to any example or role model in her own family—instead, she knew that some of the traditional "family rules" needed changing to answer some of her own personal needs. Understandably, this was difficult for her to articulate. As a way into these issues, it helped for both of them to talk about a wife's role in contemporary society.

At one point in their counseling, it was brought up that Robert always initiated sex. Janet did not feel that there was the kind of openness in their sexual relationship that would allow her to take the initiative. Robert eventually talked about his fear that Janet would become "too aggressive"—which he described as "a turn-off." But he also saw that his traditionalist view—that he should always be the initiator—limited the dimensions of their sex life. As they shared some of their own fears with each other and agreed to "try something different," some of the barriers came down. Janet was able to express her sexuality more, and Robert discovered that he could accept her initiative without feeling threatened by her in any way.

ISSUES ON WHICH TO SET RULES—AN INVENTORY

What are the issues in your relationship?

Using a separate sheet of paper respond to each of the statements below by checking "Yes" or "No." To determine your profile see the evaluation on pages 45–49. These issues are addressed at greater length in other parts of the book, and chapter references are provided in the evaluation. After you have answered, encourage your partner (without seeing your answers) to take this inventory as well.

ISSUES INVENTORY

1. "My partner and I disagree about the amount of time we should spend together."

   _____YES, this describes my relationship.

   _____NO, this does not describe my relationship.

2. "We are constantly fighting about money."

   _____YES, this describes my relationship.

   _____NO, this does not describe my relationship.

3. "We have a great deal of trouble agreeing on the chores that each of us performs around the house."

   _____YES, this describes my relationship.

   _____NO, this does not describe my relationship.

4. "We often disagree about the friends that we socialize with—either together or individually."

_____YES, this describes my relationship.

_____NO, this does not describe my relationship.

5. "We often fight about our in-laws, who seem to be interfering in our relationship."
_____YES, this describes my relationship.

_____NO, this does not describe my relationship.

6. "We're a two-career couple and have an especially difficult time tending to each of our careers and also taking care of ourselves."
_____YES, this describes my relationship.

_____NO, this does not describe my relationship.

7. "My partner and I fight a lot and have a very hard time resolving our issues."
_____YES, this describes my relationship.

_____NO, this does not describe my relationship.

8. "I have concerns that my partner or I may not stay faithful to each other."
_____YES, this describes my relationship.

_____NO, this does not describe my relationship.

9. "We have many disagreements regarding parenting (or stepparenting)."
_____YES, this describes my relationship.

_____NO, this does not describe my relationship.

10. "If I had an extramarital affair, I would not want my partner to know about it."
_____YES, this describes my relationship.

_____NO, this does not describe my relationship.

EVALUATING YOUR PROFILE

1. *"My partner and I disagree about the amount of time we should spend together."*

You may need to examine your rules about the quantity and quality of time you spend with each other. Successful couples understand each other's needs for space and privacy. Time apart does not need to detract from your relationship; in fact, your relationship can often be enhanced by privacy. Few myths are more prevalent than the one that says more togetherness equals a better relationship. (See Chapter 4).

2. *"We are constantly fighting about money."*

Arguments about financial matters in reality are often about control issues. In successful relationships, each person has his or her own amount of discretionary money, and your financial limitations as a couple become a shared problem. Watch the rule (often an unconscious rule) that says only one partner (usually the man) should control the pursestrings. This is another myth. Also, never mix issues about money with less tangible things such as sex, use of leisure time, outside friendships, and other concerns (see Chapter 4).

3. *"We have a great deal of trouble agreeing on the chores that each of us performs around the house."*

Successful couples realize that the optimal way to divide up duties is to allow each partner to be in charge of one individual area. Usually one partner is more meticulous in some respects than the other. Why not reach an agreement whereby the person who wants a particular thing done in a certain way takes responsibility for that area. Too often, one partner wastes a great deal of energy trying to get his or her partner to "comply" (see Chapter 4).

4. *"We often disagree about the friends we socialize with—either together or individually."*

Remember when you were a child and your parents tried to dictate whom you could play with? Chances are that was the first time you rebelled against parental constraints outside the home. Friends are creatures of a very special nature. Almost always, you're opening a very big can of worms if you insist that your partner stop socializing with a friend, male or female. By the same token, if one of you finds the other's friend to be distasteful, you should be able to avoid being drawn in just because you are part of a couple. If you have a friendship with someone of the same sex or someone of the opposite sex, common sense and good communication with your mate are often the best way to avoid jealousy and/or misunderstandings. Obviously, there's a big difference between staying out until 3:00 A.M. with someone who's the same sex as opposed to someone of the opposite sex. On the other side, if you suspect some romantic development between your mate and an opposite-sex friend, there's no reason why your feelings should remain hidden. Openness about your feelings as well as respect for the other's friendships are essential if each of you is to be comfortable meeting other people on your own time. Jealousy, of course, is a difficult issue—more on that in Chapter 9. Sexual partners outside the relationship are thoroughly discussed in Chapter 10.

5. *"We often fight about our in-laws, who seem to be interfering in our relationship."*

If in-laws are a problem, in all likelihood one of you is "siding" with them against the other partner. Whether or not your in-laws meant to do it, they may have found that one of you has become an ally in meeting *their* needs. For this reason it's especially important for you and your mate to discuss the communication that goes on with parents and to share in decisions about when they're invited and for how long; where you spend the holidays; and what the boundaries are of your children's relationships with grandparents.

Avoid criticizing your partner to your parents or to your in-laws. When there's a conflict in your relationship, parents are generally not good confidants, unless they have the maturity to point you back to your partner. Realize that they may not be trying to interfere on purpose. In fact, they may be completely unaware of their effect on you, and they may genuinely feel that you need emotional, moral, or financial support.

If in-laws are an ongoing problem between you, remember that either you or your partner is probably allowing them to affect you. If you and your partner are in agreement on the issues surrounding parents and in-laws, nearly all conflicts with them are resolvable (see Chapter 4).

6. *"We're a two-career couple and have an especially difficult time tending to each of our careers and also taking care of ourselves."*

Today, two-career marriages are often a necessity for financial reasons and also for greater equality in the relationship. Couples with established careers have an especially difficult time setting priorities. This situation calls for an enormous amount of mutual flexibility. Those who have established their careers and habits while living alone may find the adjustment to living together to be especially difficult (see Chapter 4).

7. *"My partner and I fight a lot and have a very hard time resolving our issues."*

If you're constantly fighting, your communication styles definitely need to be looked at. Chapters 4 and 5 may give you a great deal of insight into what might be going wrong. Often, couples fight by attacking each other at a deeply personal level, rather than dealing with the specific issue that is causing the tension. When you lose sight of the issue, not only do you fail to find a resolution but each of you contributes to the reservoir of anger.

8. *"I have concerns that my partner or I may not stay faithful to each other."*

In Chapter 10 I will describe a number of couples who have nonmonogamous living arrangements (what I call "synogamous" relationships). However, with successful couples each partner puts the other first—regardless of their arrangement.

9. *"We have many disagreements regarding parenting (or stepparenting)."*

Have a serious discussion about how each of you was brought up. Chances are the differences you discover in your own upbringing will relate directly to the differences in the ways you see raising your children. If you change those rules from "unconscious" to "spoken," you'll be in a far better position to discuss issues of child-rearing and to see where you agree and disagree with each other. Then realize that it's in your children's best interest that they have parents who (generally speaking) give them a single message. If your upbringing has been abusive in some way, you might be perpetuating similar treatment in the way you interact with your own children, or you might also react by being lenient to a fault.

The key to stepparenting is for the stepparent to have his or her own relationship with the children. In other words, the stepparent cannot rely on the child's natural parent to be a channel to the child. Developing a healthy stepparenting relationship is a slow process that requires understanding and patience. If you are a stepparent, it's essential to collaborate closely with your spouse to nurture the child. No matter what their age, children—by themselves—rarely have the maturity to make a stepparent "part of the family" (see Chapter 4).

10. *"If I had an extramarital affair, I would not want my partner to know about it."*

Today, AIDS and other sexually transmitted diseases have changed the rules for both partners. If an affair involves sexual contact without safe-sex practices then both partners may be at risk. The fact is that Robert's short trysts may be life-threatening to Janet in some circumstances. The implications of affairs and other nonmonogamous arrangements are discussed in detail in Chapter 10.

IN CONCLUSION

Rules that our parents have depended on may not work for us. On the one hand, that could mean progress. But at the same time, when we "throw out" our parents' rules, we need to develop new clarity and understanding of our own new rules. We have more choices to make, and we have more opportunities to affect our own lives and the lives of our partners.

Often, with more choice comes the pain of uncertainty as well as the adventure of trial and error. If you let yourselves explore the possibilities, you can arrive at a relationship as unique as you and your partner surely are. And there's no greater excitement than knowing that you have the ability to make changes and explore the opportunities that emerge for both of you.

CHAPTER THREE

KEEPING PASSION ALIVE

Wouldn't it be wonderful if that initial attraction never wore off? After all, in the beginning those passionate feelings usually are so effortless. That continual sense of well-being so often feels as if it will last forever.

If passion and comfort are the two main pillars of a love relationship, think of passion as the spark that kindles the relationship and will keep things going for a period of time. As a relationship moves out of that initial phase, reality takes the place of the fantasy that may once have made your relationship feel like a living romance novel. Gradually, your partner becomes a *real* person to you, and your relationship—if it is to survive—needs to become integrated with both of your lives. During this evolutionary process, you begin to develop feelings for your partner that expand far beyond the fulfillment of sexual and romantic needs. Gradually, as you begin to recognize your partner as a person (as well as a love object), you are likely to see that both of you have a wide range of needs to fulfill. This is the slow and gradual process by which comfort and familiarity are developed. It is this process that makes longevity possible in the relationship.

At this point, most couples begin to notice a decrease in the driving passion that first may have brought them together.

The story often goes like this: "It seems as though as soon as we decided to move in together, our sex life took a nosedive," said Deborah and Jim at the couple's first counseling session. "It's not as though it was smooth sailing up to that point, either. We had lots of issues around making a commitment to each other and getting used to each other's idiosyncrasies. But as soon as we thought we were through all of that, something happened to our passion. For the first time, if we were angry at each other about something, we would carry it over into the bedroom."

At first, Jim almost could not get enough sex, but then he began to lose interest. Deborah and Jim actually panicked as a result of this phenomenon and began to give their decision to live together second thoughts. They needed only to understand the nature of their unreal expectation that their initial attraction and its by-product—passion—would continue at the same level of intensity forever.

On the other hand, Cheryl and Alan saw a marked decrease in their desire for each other after the birth of their first child. Both of them felt overburdened with their new responsibilities. Alan felt neglected and resentful. Cheryl reacted to this by being sexually unavailable. For each of them, this was a second marriage. Cheryl talked of her experience as being reminiscent of how she had lost desire for her first husband during a period of extreme financial difficulties. Alan confided to me that he was beginning to have thoughts of going outside of the marriage for sexual fulfillment, which he'd done in his first marriage but did not want to do again.

For Cheryl and Alan to begin to resolve their problem, they had to learn how to keep anger from interfering with their sexual activities.

Passion has both its positive and negative sides. In this

chapter, we're going to focus on enhancing passion. This includes the sexual, romantic, and playful aspects of your relationship. In Chapter 5, we will take a look at how passion can be negative when it is the driving force behind stormy relationships. As we will see, many stormy relationships are those that, at their worst, become "brain dead" while remaining "heart alive." In these it is important to develop other aspects. However, increasing passion is generally necessary to prevent a relationship from becoming "heart dead" even though it may be very comfortable and very much "brain alive."

The main problem most couples have in working toward increasing their passion for each other is acknowledging that this side of their relationship needs to be worked on at all. In my experience, many couples have no problem admitting they need help with financial, in-law, or child-rearing problems, but they find the idea of working at staying lovers to be totally abhorrent. While there is some truth to the adage "either it's there or it's not there" when talking about initial attraction, that's not the case when it comes to established relationships.

Jane and Steve have been married twenty-five years. They have two grown children and still very much enjoy each other sexually. I asked them how they have managed to keep their passion alive after all this time. "We stay closely in touch with each other's feelings and moods. If I feel distant, I'll tell Jane that and we talk about it," Steve said. Jane added that "at first it felt risky to talk about my feelings, but now I can't imagine it any other way. We have a definite need to be near and close to each other, and that's because we each find it nourishing. By being open we have developed a level of trust that certainly wasn't there at the beginning."

Both Jane and Steve assured me that theirs isn't a storybook romance either. Steve admitted, "We don't have sex as often as we once did, but we are just as affectionate. If one of us isn't into it, we don't let it be a problem. Neither of us feels rejected or too sensitive about it. It took us a long time, but we feel no shame toward each other, and we constantly experiment. We rarely let anger hold over to the next day, and we don't attempt sex when we are angry." According to Jane,

"We've been through some tough periods, and without that communication we wouldn't have made it this far. But now, I can't imagine anything we couldn't handle."

Some of the other discoveries Jane and Steve found helpful include beginning their foreplay before entering the bedroom, when possible—sometimes even beginning the anticipation hours beforehand by using the type of sexy talk each of them likes. They also sincerely compliment each other's bodies—both verbally and by doing a lot of touching—and have often gone to motels for the purpose of lovemaking when it was hard or impossible to relax sexually because of the constant pressure of kids.

Jane and Steve demonstrate a climate that almost any couple can achieve if they are willing to focus on and attend to this area of their relationship.

Clearly, when the task at hand involves increasing passion, the symptoms that you and your partner need to recognize include the following:

• You have passed the initial stage of your relationship, and the beginning chemistry has worn off and passion is no longer *automatic* as it once was. Yet there is the desire (at least the intellectual commitment) to stay together and work toward long-term involvement.

• When you feel noticeably less excited sexually by your partner and this becomes a source of concern for either of you, or when your partner feels less excited by you.

• When some life change such as the birth of a child; a change in career, job, or financial status; a crisis or choice in some other part of your life is followed by or coincides with a decrease in either your sexual appetite or your ability to have fun together in other ways that you once shared.

• When an ongoing issue (such as a disagreement you cannot seem to get resolved) produces chronic anger or unhappiness for either of you, particularly if one of you feels like a loser in the situation.

• If either one of you is experiencing one of the sexual dysfunctions such as inhibited or total loss of sexual desire, premature ejaculation, impotence, anorgasmia, or vaginismus (see discussion of these later in the chapter).

• If your sexual energies are directed outside of the relationship and this is not your choice. (In Chapter 10, we'll talk about situations in which this is your choice.)

• Where either you or your partner is feeling turned off by what you perceive as your partner's insensitivity toward your needs (or vice versa).

• If you are avoiding being alone together or picking petty fights with each other when you are, and you don't really know why.

• If there is a troubling difference in the amount of affection as well as sex that either of you desires.

• If at some point you realize that sex (or sex that's pleasurable) is slowly becoming more and more a thing of the past.

> ## SOME SIMPLE
> ## FACTS ABOUT SEX

No matter which you put first, there are really two master reasons why we have sex: to provide a vehicle for *pleasure* and for *procreation*. Yet, sadly, sex for so many has become a form of control, manipulation, pain, humiliation, contest, self-esteem, or lack thereof. In addition, it's been known to trigger just about every emotion—positive or negative—known to mankind. We have created many myths about sex and so often have used our sexuality to define our entire self-image (not to mention the value of our entire relationship) in either a positive or a negative way.

Sexual response is now one of the most studied aspects of human behavior. While we don't know all the answers, there are a few things we do know. So before going any further, see if you can apply some of these well-accepted facts—intended to demystify sex—to your situation:

• It is very rare, perhaps impossible, to find two people for whom sex means exactly the same thing or who experience it in exactly the same way. For example, once the dust settles and that initial chemistry fades, it is a rare couple who desires the same *amount* of sex. This does not make the one who wants more "more in love," nor does it mean that the one who wants less is more distant, less intimate, or less committed.

• What one finds to be pleasurable or distasteful is a highly individual matter as well. Thus, the first step is to accept within yourself your own desires. The next step is to communicate them to your partner. It goes without saying that once communicated, acknowledging your partner's desires is essential. What are some ways to acknowledge a partner's sexual desire? How can you remain open to sexual exploration and discovery in the way that Jane and Steve have done in their relationship?

In this regard, imagination and a willingness to listen to your partner are both important. Often, it's important to *ask* ("Shall we go to a motel this weekend and get away from the kids?"). And, having asked, to be ready to explore what your partner wants ("Not a motel—but if we could just go out to dinner somewhere . . .").

Be aware that your partner's tastes may change too. Ask for what *you* want—and don't be surprised if your needs are quite different! When each of you is aware of what feels good to the other person, both of you can derive a great deal of pleasure, satisfaction, and intimacy from the pleasure you give to each other.

• Don't expect sex to be necessarily spontaneous. While spontaneity is much more likely to occur frequently in the beginning, life often gets too complex later on to rely on that. With the normal fatigue and the humdrum demands of busy lives, many couples actually need to make definite plans and set aside time to be together sexually. This is particularly true when you have children and complicated work schedules. Take it for granted that sex will require more planning than it did during that wonderful period of courtship, when all you had to do when you were together was to attend to your own and each other's needs.

• Make sure that your expectations are realistic. For example, it's okay to actually be a little *less* attracted to your partner as familiarity increases. Be aware, too, that physiological changes over time affect both men and women sexually. These are all normal changes, so don't take them as "sure signs" of the demise of your relationship. It's more important (as well as effective) that you adjust your expectations.

• Don't compare your desires or your partner's preferences with the "norms" of sexual behavior that show up in media images. There *are* things that we know to be true. For example, practically everyone has sexual fantasies, sexual anxieties, sexual preferences, and different ideas about how important sex is. Other than that, the information you hear that's valid will generally take individual differences into consideration. With the exception of a small fringe of couples who engage in the type of sexual practices that can result in injury or death, nothing between consenting adults is problematic unless either partner says it is. Some couples enjoy being creative sexually, while others are perfectly happy being more conventional. I have met many who thought they were sexually inept as a result of their experience in one relationship who found a comfortable and exciting situation in another.

• Keeping the above in mind, one can see how most sexual problems are resolved. As one couple once said in my office at the conclusion of their treatment, "Things started getting much better for us sexually when we really started practicing 'oral sex'—that is, we began talking about it as well as doing it."

A sexual problem that affects one partner is a sexual problem for the couple. So, in that spirit, keep these approaches in mind regarding your sexual needs:

• If you and your partner differ in the amount of sex you each desire, work out a compromise that, at times, lets the one who wants sex less frequently be more passively involved. (Examples are: watching your partner masturbate or providing your partner only with manual stimulation.) By the same token, the one who desires more sex needs to back off at times without interpreting the other partner's lack of response or different mood as a rejection.

• Birth control methods are the responsibility of *both* partners. There is no universal pat solution here, but couples who don't want to conceive can usually find ways to preserve pleasure for both partners. Just be sure to talk about it—so that you know what you and your partner *do* find pleasurable and so that you can "work around" the limitations of whatever contraceptive method you use.

• In communicating sexual desires or sexual concerns (whether about intercourse, birth control, masturbation, etc.), each partner needs to make a commitment to the other to be honest. This is the type of honesty that helps you to build intimacy. If it can be achieved at this level, that intimacy will spill over to other areas of your relationship as well. Try to share more and more things about yourself and your desires. Take the opportunity to reveal your sexual fantasies as well. Remember, no one was ever hurt by a sexual fantasy—kept at the level of fantasy or imagination—no matter how "unrealistic" the fantasy might be. In other words, give yourself permission to explore your and your partner's fantasy life without feeling threatened. At the level of imagination, you can explore whatever is enjoyable to both of you.

• Leave anger out of the bedroom. If something is bothering you so much that it gets in the way of your sex life, deal with that issue first. If you find you are unable to resolve the issue, I recommend that you seek couples' therapy or counseling. Don't let unresolved and often unrelated issues poison your sex life. If you do, it will only be a matter of time before your relationship hits a real (and perhaps irreparable) crisis.

• Part of communicating your sexual desires is not only to *tell* but to *show* your partner what it is that you prefer. I call this teaching your partner *visceral empathy*. As individuals, each of us differs in the amount of touch we like, how we like to be touched (such as with more or less pressure), where we like to be touched (those spots we find very pleasurable, too sensitive, or downright painful), and the different points in our lovemaking at which we like certain things to be done. Some people like or love oral sex, others don't. Some like to talk during sex, some find it a turnoff. Some people like to remain physically close for a while after sex, while others prefer to be left alone.

No one can possibly be expected to know these things about you without your help. If your partner isn't satisfying you, don't make matters worse by casting blame. Instead, assume that by teaching your partner how to satisfy you and by your reciprocating, you will get to know each other and grow together in this area. Think of your lovemaking as a type of deal: "You please me and, in return, I will please you." Never think of yourself as a martyr or someone who only gives in this way "altruistically." If you begin feeling that way, it's probably a good indication that you need to say to your partner: "I'm not getting what I need from our sex life. Can we talk about it?" (And this could be the perfect opportunity for your partner to talk about his or her needs as well.)

• There is no lack of information on lovemaking techniques. Alex Comfort's *The Joy of Sex* and many books like it will give you numerous ideas about sexual exploration that you can try together. If you seek out such information with an eagerness to experiment, you may discover many wonderful adventures with your partner. Variations of foreplay and sex are infinite— and your partner may be as excited by these variations as you are. You owe it to yourselves to learn about some of them.

• Sexual and sensual play does not mean only intercourse. It refers to any type of physical intimacy that you and your partner share. For some partners, watching a sexy or romantic movie may be a pleasurable way to establish intimacy; for others, a quiet conversation about the day's events, or the recollection of a moment you shared, might bring you much closer to one another. Taking a bath together, massaging, kissing, and touching—all these sensations can become part of a pleasurable sexual experience. Variety, for many couples, is key.

And keep in mind: even though a pleasurable sexual encounter can include orgasm for either person, it does not necessarily have to.

• When communicating your sexual needs, if you still find yourself holding back, try to understand what your issues and fears are. Are you telling yourself that your partner should *know* what to do for you even though you don't ask? (That would be mental telepathy!) Do you fear embarrassment? Do you fear being judged negatively for talking about fantasies that may be a little different from desires you've labeled as normal? Please keep in mind that you are the only authority on your sexual and sensual needs, and your partner is the one person who can say what pleases him or her.

When discussing the fulfillment or acting out of each other's sexual fantasies, consider these special points:

• Always discuss limits beforehand, and make sure that you thoroughly resolve your disagreements about those limits.

• Develop some code word to say "this is enough"; before proceeding, make sure that you each agree to stop at any time if the other person wants to. If you try something that you find to be unpleasant, you may choose to try it a different way next time or simply agree not to repeat it.

• Never allow yourself to be forced or force your partner to do anything that may produce guilt or other residual negative feelings. Each of you needs to allow the other person the right to consent or not at any time.

• Feel free to use your imagination so that each of you can have the opportunity to introduce new roles; this exploration will make the experience special for both of you. Be aware, however, that many people find that acting out a fantasy is less enjoyable than relishing it in the imagination. So, for some, there's truth to the adage that "the greatest aphrodisiac of all is your own mind."

SEXUAL DYSFUNCTIONS

Up to now, our discussion about sex has focused on your choices. If one or both of you has a sexual dysfunction, on the other hand, your choices will be limited because a partner is unable (as opposed to unwilling) to perform sexually. Many people experience occasional sexual difficulties that are short-term in nature. But if a condition continues to the point where it seems to be a consistent problem, I urge you to seek professional help. When it becomes apparent that your ongoing satisfaction is being prevented by sexual dysfunction, the assistance of a professional can be extremely helpful. The success rate in therapy for most sexual dysfunctions is high. Often such therapy involves a combination of psychotherapy and/or medical intervention. In-depth discussion of the common sexual dysfunctions can be found in many fine self-help books, but is beyond the scope of this one. I list the dysfunctions here to help you recognize the problem, should it occur.

INHIBITED SEXUAL DESIRE

ISD, as it's called, is extremely common. Its symptom, a marked decrease in sexual desire, can affect either or both members of a couple. In addition, ISD may be directed only toward your partner, or it could exclude any type of sexual feelings at all. In the former case, this is usually symptomatic of a problem within the relationship; in the latter case, ISD can be caused by a combination of psychological and medical factors. ISD is never to be confused with the difference in the amount of sex one partner or the other desires. Instead, it refers to the difference between what was once your norm compared to what it is now. ISD may be a chronic condition, or it may be sporadic. At its extreme, it can mean a total loss of desire.

PREMATURE EJACULATION

The man lacks control and ejaculates very quickly (in less than one to three minutes) after penetration, and sometimes even before penetration. There are some very clear-cut procedures that can be learned in therapy to improve this condition in a short period of time.

IMPOTENCE

This generally refers to a male's inability to achieve erection or to perform. (Again, he may lose his erection before penetration or soon afterwards.) A man with *primary impotence* has never been able to perform sexually. *Secondary impotence* is the diagnosis if a man was once able to perform sexually, but has lost a degree of that ability.

EJACULATORY INCOMPETENCE

A man who has this dysfunction cannot ejaculate during intercourse. Instead, during intercourse he maintains an erection for an inordinately long period of time.

ANORGASMIA

Applies to a woman who has never been able to achieve orgasm—or who can achieve orgasm only under certain circumstances, such as when masturbating. If she cannot have an orgasm with her partner in a way that she finds satisfactory, she may have a degree of this condition.

VAGINISMUS

A tightening of the vagina to a degree that does not allow penetration during intercourse.

DYSPARUNIA

Painful intercourse: It can occur in men or women, but is much more common in women.

Sexual dysfunction can have many causes. Among them are unresolved issues in the relationship, early sexual conditioning, negative body image, lack of adequate sexual stimulation, or an actual medical problem. One very common cause is *performance anxiety*, which can affect either a man or a woman.

Typically, someone who has performance anxiety feels "turned off" just before the sexual act is about to begin, with anxiety thought to be the underlying feeling. Any of these causes—or a combination of them—can contribute to total or partial loss of sexual appetite or to a loss of the ability to perform. Once a sexual dysfunction occurs, it often takes on a life of its own: Increased performance anxiety only increases the fear of another sexual failure. But, remember, a great deal is known about all of the above dysfunctions. I always feel sad when a couple tells me that it has taken them years to seek information or treatment for a problem that bothered either or both of them. Once addressed, such a problem might be easily corrected in a matter of weeks or months.

OTHER WAYS TO INCREASE PASSION

Though sex is an extremely important element of passion, it is certainly not all there is. Passion is what made you a couple in the first place, and what makes your relationship special. And yet, what couple does not feel passion ebbing away at times? Passion is what makes you want to be with each other.

What are the keys to keeping passion alive? There are no guarantees, of course, but the partners who seem to share the most passion also have these things in common:

• When sex is going well, often it's taken for granted. But when it isn't working, it can be a very painful factor in your relationship. Couples who remember the importance of communication are often the best at keeping sexual passion alive. I recommend that you attend to your sex life when either of you recognizes that a problem exists. And, as I've recommended, seek professional help if you can't address the problem by yourselves.

• They address anger rather than letting it "seethe." Anger generated by unresolved issues can zap away your desire for each other. If this is the case, first concentrate on resolving the issues about which you are angry. (See the next two chapters.) In most cases, that will make a huge difference.

• They enjoy nonsexual play together. This is also an important part of most relationships. Do you spend time together doing some of the things that you enjoyed early in your relationship? You know what you like or liked doing together (giving each other massages; attending movies, plays, and concerts; playing scrabble; taking walks; going horseback riding, sitting by the fire, going to the beach, etc., etc., etc.). Yet these are the activities that most frequently get neglected in the whirlwind of life. Don't let that happen. Set the time aside for things you *like* to do as well as things you *must* do together. Learn to laugh more together. Learn more about each other. Share more aspects of yourself with your partner. Keep increasing your intimacy level by letting life's events bring you closer, not farther apart.

When passion dies, it is rarely one person's fault. If you see this happening, take the responsibility to work together to restore it. That very process itself may be the thing that brings passion—and you—back together.

CHAPTER FOUR

COMMUNICA-TION STYLES

How often I hear this complaint from couples: "We don't communicate."

They do, of course. To some degree, every couple communicates constantly. (Even "the silent treatment" is a powerful form of communication!) So what they're really talking about is the *quality* of communication. Is it superb, merely adequate, or just plain abysmal? To the extent that you and your partner spend time together, communication goes on constantly. But you may often wonder how well you actually understand each other's means of communication.

In this chapter, we're going to look at overall communication—what it is, its implications, and how to improve it in all of the areas of your relationship.

Communication in marriage and other love relationships has for many years been the subject of much ongoing research. What the findings generally have shown is that the best indicator of whether a couple will stay together is the degree to which they communicate effectively. For couples who communicate well, establishing *comfort*, the pillar most associated with longevity, is a natural by-product. Establishing comfort is that process whereby you get to know more and more about just *who* that person you've chosen to be your partner *is* and how you can actually build together the lives that you once dreamed about as your relationship continued to grow.

Unlike that nebulous yet unmistakable aura we call passion, *good communication can be learned.* That's the good news! Once you learn to communicate effectively, you can apply communication skills to every aspect of your relationship. Almost any crisis can be handled—even the ones that seem to jeopardize your relationship—if you can communicate well.

"Until Shawn got laid off, we communicated beautifully," said Barbara, his wife, during their first session. "Sure, we had our arguments. In fact, when we were first married, we used to fight quite a bit, but we were always able to make up. Why is it that when he lost his job, we just stopped talking?"

Barbara and Shawn were to find out those means of communication they had relied on until a crisis came along were not adequate to withstand the new stress. They hadn't learned how to support each other through a crisis because they had never before confronted a problem of this magnitude during their relationship. When crises are precipitated by such high-stress events as financial problems, a sudden move, illness or a death in the family, it's not uncommon to find that communication suffers as a result.

How can we communicate better with our partner on a day-to-day basis, so we stay in touch with their thoughts, needs, and feelings? And how can we keep communication flowing when we most need to—during times of high stress that tax our emotional resources?

One way to communicate more effectively is by developing alternative attitudes that can make us more open to our partners. If you have some of the "old attitudes" in the following lists, can you begin to develop some of the "alternative attitudes" that might improve communication with your partner?

• *Old Attitude:* "There is something I really want to share with my partner, but I feel uncomfortable doing so."

Alternative Attitude: "I have chosen my partner. We are intimate in many other ways. My relationship is important enough to me to risk being more open." (Think of risk-taking as an exercise in which you can't really lose. If things work out for you, it's easy to see how you've gotten what you want. But even if the risk turns out to yield the worst possible results, then you've learned a great deal about your partner, your relationship—as it now stands—and what may gravely need attention from both of you, if you are to stay together.)

• *Old Attitude:* "It's easier to let things go than to deal with the disagreement that will follow if I share my feelings."

Alternative Attitude: "It would be nice if something I'd like to avoid really would go away that easily, but I know in my heart of hearts that it will only come up again, so I am better off facing it now."

• *Old Attitude:* "I'm always the one who wants to talk when there is an issue. Therefore, I must be more vested in the relationship than my partner."

Alternative Attitude: "Like differences in sex drive, it's a rare relationship in which each partner has the same need to share issues. I accept this as another of our individual differences."

• *Old Attitude:* "I've given up telling my partner about things that are bothering me. Whenever I do, my partner jumps in to tell me what I should have done differently. I end up feeling negated, overwhelmed, and sorry I ever brought the subject up in the first place."

Alternative Attitude: "This is something that had better be talked about independently of our other issues." (People who jump in and act as rescuers—and who may even have the tendency to finish your sentences for you—generally don't realize how what they're doing is affecting you. If you explain to your partner a few times—in a calm yet assertive way and direct way—it will help your partner to see what he or she is doing.)

• *Old Attitude:* "Whenever I ask my partner what he or she feels about an issue or something we're discussing, my partner generally answers, 'I don't know.' This frustrates me."

Alternative Attitude: "I need to look at my own communication style as well as my partner's." (Some people do not easily respond to the question "What are you feeling?" Instead, try: "What are you thinking?" or "What do you think about . . . ?" Your partner may find it more natural to relate cognitively to concrete facts or to thoughts rather than to feelings. Many couples differ in the way they perceive situations. One partner may relate intellectually, while the other puts a greater emphasis on feelings. This difference is a problem only when either tries to make the other wrong.)

> ## COMMUNICATION
> ## AVOIDANCE 101

In addition to your attitudes about communication, your style is important. Following are some actual styles of communication—conversing, discussing, or even fighting—that tend to be traps. Perhaps these communication styles have been developed over a long period of time; if so, they may be difficult to break. But not impossible. To the extent that any of these patterns characterize the way you and your partner normally communicate, especially about difficult subjects, chances are you are spinning your wheels.

Here are twelve typical ways communication is ultimately stifled. See if any of them apply to you.

1. *Drowning in anger.* One of you tries to discuss an issue while the other is ventilating anger. This doesn't work! I have yet to see an important matter resolved in any meaningful way during the heat of an argument.

2. *Defensiveness.* One of you becomes angry or defensive when confronted by an issue. Then, instead of dealing with the issue at hand, you have an *emotional reaction* to the issue— and *that* is the reaction that takes over. When you finally calm

down, perhaps it becomes excruciatingly desirable just to "forget" what you were arguing about originally and to soothe each other's emotions instead. Since the problem still lingers, just waiting for the next triggering event or conversation, nothing is resolved.

There's another variation: many couples become passionate and sensual after an argument, even though the real source of tension still hangs over them. Thus, anger becomes an antecedent to passionate sex. But when the sex is over, the original issue remains intact and continues to nag at your relationship.

3. *Blatant avoidance.* How often does one of you leave the house, go to another room, or simply turn a deaf ear to the other? This halted communication triggers a negative effect— and then the situation is likely to snowball until neither of you can talk about what's wrong.

4. *Right issue, wrong time.* An issue that is brought up at an inappropriate time, such as when one partner is on the way to work, is unlikely to receive much attention. If there is company present or the children are around, you can be certain that you and your partner will not have much opportunity to deal straightforwardly with an issue.

5. *Rigidity.* Either or both of you have the need to be "right" one hundred percent of the time. When that's the situation, you're not achieving much clarity, because someone is always trying to win.

6. *Being too personal.* Attacking your partner's character or personality rather than focusing on the specifics of the issue.

7. *Not letting go.* While fighting about one thing, you bring up old issues (probably some that are even "resolved") that you use to "justify" your position now.

8. *All or nothing.* You put your entire relationship on the line over every single disagreement and then wonder why either partner avoids anything that smacks of a confrontation.

9. *Allowing a lethal buildup.* Is either of you a "pleaser"? If you're quick to agree on practically everything, you may let your real feelings build and build until a slight issue "lights your fuse"—and a nonissue turns into a major crisis. In other

words, you may be allowing your fear of confrontation to dominate your communication style. If you pretend things are fine when they're really not, anger is likely to build. If you're a pleaser, you may be deep into the relationship before you show your partner the first signs of that anger. But all along, you and your partner are dealing with the buildup of emotions rather than the actual issues that are prompting those emotions.

10. *Top dog/underdog.* Arguments become exercises in control, with one or both of you trying to wear the other down. Here, the real but unspoken goal for either of you could be to gain control of the other.

11. *The forest for the trees.* You say you're "not communicating," but really mean that your partner is telling you what you don't want to hear.

12. *"You're all alike . . ."* Either of you devalues the other one by attributing your conflict or one partner's stand to the partner's sex. For example, you say, "Wo/men . . . are so insensitive in this area," or you attack by pointing to your partner's religion, ethnic background, family, age, the norms of your partner's family of origin, etc., etc., etc., rather than staying with the issue or acknowledging your partner's ability to be free of any stereotype.

As you may have noticed, the possible combinations are numerous. Imagine how difficult it is to resolve an issue positively when a "pleaser" meets a "top dog" or when two "all or nothing" partners get together! In fact, most couples develop a blend of various styles of avoidance that then become uniquely their own.

It is a rare couple that doesn't resort to some of the above patterns at times. But any of these negative communication styles can undo many of the good things you have together if they are how you typically communicate, especially when the going gets tough. I recommend that both you and your partner go through this list together and ask yourselves, "Is that us?" And if you do get a shock of recognition at some of these communication problems, discuss how you can get around these obstacles. If you both see the need to work together toward more effective communication, you've already taken a big step. Talking about *how* you communicate (communicating about communicating!) is a great way to begin modeling new patterns in your relationship.

> ## COMMUNICATION STYLES THAT WORK

Effective communicating simply means reaching your partner with a message you really want heard and, just as importantly, *reciprocating* by hearing when he or she reaches out. Good communicaiton does a number of things. It not only gets your message across, but also makes the other person *want* to hear your point of view and perhaps consider changing certain habits or clarifying some attitudes that may have become a source of tension in your relationship.

To get back on track, you might use some of the following guides to constructive communication.

GIVING FEEDBACK

When you give feedback, be as specific as possible. Good feedback is focused on behavior and things *that can be changed* in the other person. It's given in a constructive manner, instead of in such a way as to cause your partner to react defensively. Good feedback is based on observations—not judgment. An example of *bad* feedback would be to tell your partner that he or she is a nasty person. Such a heavy judgment will nearly always lead to a defensive response. A more effective alternative would be to say, "You seem angry, but I don't understand what you're angry about." Wouldn't the latter statement be more likely to give your partner room to make his or her feeling better known, rather than forcing your partner to defend certain behavior?

Feedback can be particularly effective in confronting your partner's blind spots. The fact is, your partner may be unaware of behavior that you find annoying or hard to live with. By helping your partner to recognize your feelings about that behavior, rather than merely *attacking* it, you will go much further toward resolving the source of upset or conflict. It's the difference between saying, "I don't like *you* when you're angry" and, "I don't like the way *I feel* [or it feels] when there is a climate of anger and hostility." The first is an attack on your partner; the second is an expression of your own feelings.

COMMUNICATING ASSERTIVELY

There is no limit to how an issue can be mishandled. Some couples seem capable only of arguing angrily and *aggressively* with the aim of putting each other down. Worse yet, they act out their anger by doing things to hurt each other. Other couples believe that the "solution" is to avoid the matter completely. In the middle there's the happy medium that works. It's called *assertive* communication. That is where your feelings are expressed in words, but without threatening, putting down, or overpowering your partner.

It is particularly important not only to share but to take responsibility for your feelings. When communicating assertively, make "I" statements. Instead of saying, "You never listen to me," try saying, "I wish that you were more responsive when I talk to you about things that are important to me." Instead of, "You are insensitive," say, "I am hurt by . . ." By making "I" statements, you do much to reduce the chance that your partner will feel attacked and then react defensively. As you probably have experienced yourself when attacked, a natural reaction is to be defensive. When you or your partner becomes defensive, you actually avoid the issue in such a way that reinforces your anger and continues the vicious cycle. When you express your feelings in an assertive manner, you avoid starting this cycle.

Assertive communication is the alternative to the angry climate where one or both of you devalue each other. On the other hand, being *non*assertive (that is, pretending the issue doesn't exist or pretending to be unaffected) does not make the feeling disappear. It merely ensures that you will continue to stew with unexpressed anger. This quite common and negative process can poison every aspect of your relationship and can affect your health.

So, if assertive communication is so good, why do people resist it? It could be *fear*. Perhaps you fear that you'll open a Pandora's box of complaints and counter-complaints if you begin being assertive. Sometimes the fear relates to what may have happened when you asserted yourself in a past relationship. Perhaps you even fear being abandoned by your partner for being assertive. However, usually when you learn to communicate assertively, you find that the results are not destructive as you may have feared. And there is always a "hidden cost" in being nonassertive—the cost of hiding what you really think and feel (that is, who you really are) from your partner.

FACT OR FEELING

While feelings are not absolute facts, they do factually describe what is going on inside someone. Thus, if your partner tells you, "I feel angry at you because you were very unresponsive to me," what is most important is not so much whether or not you were unresponsive but the fact that your partner *feels* that way.

By the same token, you can't really change your partner's feelings. If you say, "You are wrong to feel that way," you may be headed on a course of frustration. Can you, instead, just acknowledge your partner's feelings without trying to change them? Remember, when it comes to our feelings, we all have our own realities.

By acknowledging and reacting sensitively to your partner's feelings, you have the power to make a dramatic change in the emotional climate that exists between the two of you. Acknowledging your partner's feelings is not to be confused with giving in. Think of it as a way of holding up your share of the responsibility for communication. In addition, being assertive also involves asking for what you want *without the attitude that you shouldn't have to ask. Never* expect your partner to be a mind-reader. With some work, understanding, and practice, your efforts will likely be reciprocated, and you'll be able to handle most issues together.

LISTENING

You are *really* listening when you are hearing the *spirit* in which something is being said to you as well as the *literal words*.

Rarely have I met anyone who has complained about their own ability to listen; but many are quick to complain about their *partners'* listening habits. Sometimes it's easier to illustrate what listening is *not*.

You are probably not listening when you're giving advice or just gathering data so you *can* give advice. And you're certainly not listening when you tell your partner that he or she should not feel a certain way.

On the other hand, you're not necessarily listening when you're just trying to soothe feelings or smooth over troubled waters. Indeed, that can be just another form of negating your partner's feelings.

Whether your partner is being rational or irrational, telling you something you want to hear or don't want to hear, listening is simply *taking it in*. To be truly good at listening, try to ask questions or make comments *only* to clarify what the speaker is saying. You will get your chance to react to the actual content of the message later on. But the first task of listening is to make certain you know what you are responding to.

The following exercise is one that many couples find quite helpful as they learn to listen to each other.

Set aside thirty minutes with your partner. During the first ten minutes, ask your partner to talk to you about something he or she would like you to know and understand. During this period, limit your own responses: only try to clarify what your partner is saying. If you make comments, do so only at times when a response is clearly asked for.

After ten minutes, take a few minutes to share with your

partner what you heard. Then switch roles. You now become the speaker and let your partner become the listener. Now you will be in control of the conversation during the next ten-minute segment. After that, during the remaining time, it's your partner's turn to say what he or she heard. You may be surprised during the give-and-take of this process at how differently you heard each other. I encourage you to try to define some of the distinctions in your individual listening styles: it may help you understand why you or your partner may sometimes feel as though you're not "getting through" to the other.

Most couples report that sitting back and listening—if that's what their partner calls for—was at first very difficult. However, once they've learned how to do that, overall communication becomes a lot easier and more pleasant. You can repeat this exercise, of course—and it's especially important to do so when you feel yourselves slipping. Feel free to vary the time you allot for segments—as long as you *both* have a chance to "practice your listening" (i.e., letting your partner talk) during the time you set aside.

SOME COMMON ISSUES OF A NORMAL RELATIONSHIP

It's quite predictable that the partner who is in the worst pain is the one who wants to communicate the most about any given issue. But what can plague a relationship? The possibilities are infinite! It's a rare relationship that at one time or another doesn't have a sticky issue that needs some special attention. The following are some of the more common ones.

FINANCES

No longer do sex-role stereotypes determine how your finances are handled. In many relationships, negotiating what will be satisfactory to both partners can be very time-consuming. However, most couples will get through this if they are willing to be flexible.

It is important to set up a plan that has two important elements: (1) fixed and mutual expenses are covered; and (2) each person has an agreed-upon amount of discretionary money that can be spent without giving the other partner an explanation. The earlier in the relationship that you set up this two-part plan, the better. Problems usually arise when the one who makes more money assumes an attitude of control that becomes a focus of the other partner's resentment. This is especially common in two-income families where earnings are unequal.

Often it works well for one partner to be in charge of the financial logistics, such as paying the bills and taking care of taxes, etc. However, both partners usually want to feel that they are part of the decision-making; both usually need to understand how money is allocated and spent. In a two-income family, many couples find that it works best if both contribute agreed-upon amounts to the common expenses. Individual finances are kept separate for each partner and remain under his or her own control.

IN-LAWS

Yes, in-laws can interfere dramatically with a married couple—and sometimes their influence is unintentional. In most cases, they truly "want the best for you." It's important for you and your partner to agree that you will not ask for opinions or advice from either set of parents, if you don't want it. This especially applies to issues and arguments that would be best kept between you and your partner. If your family criticizes your partner, it could be because you are airing some of your dirty laundry to them. If you must go outside your relationship for a confidant, don't make it a parent. (Few parents are wise enough to point you back to your partner to work things out.) Most importantly, parents will often reinforce your anger and take sides themselves and then remain angry long after the two of you have patched things up.

If you've been depending on parents for financial support or assistance with some expenses, don't blame them completely if they try to be too "helpful." They may genuinely believe that you need emotional and moral support as well. It's your responsibility to separate emotionally from your family of origin—not their responsibility to "free" you! And what applies to parents often applies to stepparents, other relatives, and even close friends.

STEPPARENTING ISSUES

Whenever you or your partner have children from a previous marriage, the relationship inherits a special set of issues.

If your partner is to be a stepparent to your children, it is extremely important that you allow your partner and your children to form their own relationship. In other words, do everything possible *not* to be in the middle. Often, this is a tough adjustment for everyone, but well worth the effort. If your partner and your children can learn to work through their own conflicts, there will be less potential for hidden resentment on either side.

Meanwhile, with your partner, try to negotiate just how much responsibility and authority your partner has over the children. For instance, does your partner have the authority to discipline? Is your partner expected to share the children's expenses? Are the children to be taken along on vacations? What is the stepparent to be called? (Mom or Dad? By his or her first name?) Who will be the parent consulted when it comes to making decisions about school, camp, and other inevitable matters—will it be your partner or the children's other natural parent?

Whether one or both of you are bringing children into the relationship, it's important to be very clear about the day-to-day arrangements. Are the children with you full-time or only on weekends and special occasions? What is the children's relationship with their other parent? Just how active a stepparent does your partner want to be?

In my experience, couples who have the most difficulty being stepparents are those who don't take these matters into consideration until they become full-blown problems. I have seen some couples, who after discussing these matters thoroughly, have decided that marriage or a live-in relationship just won't work. However, they are able to continue a long-term relationship by *not* trying to blend two households into one—and they have agreed to keep children out of their relationship as much as possible. Other couples find the presence of stepchildren to be an added bonus they never realized they would enjoy so much. This is true especially when one partner has no children of his or her own, yet now enjoys having a relationship with a partner's child or children.

Needless to say, blended families don't click overnight. In addition to rivalries between children and stepparents, there are sometimes rivalries between the stepparent and the natural parent counterpart—either spoken or unspoken.

Be realistic: Expect a sometimes slow transition period where it's normal for each player to feel a bit like an outsider before everyone gets comfortable with their new roles. I say this again because it warrants repeating: *As hard as it is, whenever possible, let your partner and your children form their own relationships and settle their own conflicts.*

TWO-CAREER RELATIONSHIPS

Partners who each have meaningful careers sometimes find it difficult to compromise on issues that were once determined by sex-role stereotypes. In addition, a career-driven individual who has lived alone often finds the adjustment to living together to be extremely difficult. It's sometimes impossible for optimum career opportunities to be pursued by both partners simultaneously, particularly when advancement involves relocating. In fact, the entire relationship may be thrown into crisis. In addition, managing two separate careers makes other decisions—such as having children (see Chapter 12)—equally difficult.

LONG-DISTANCE RELATIONSHIPS

These are becoming more and more common. There's one bonus: In a long-distance relationship, the partners may find it much easier to resist fighting about trivial issues. Some studies have found that couples who have long-distance love affairs actually put more energy and thought into maintaining their relationship than do those who live in closer proximity. In addition, and for obvious reasons, partners who live great distances from each other are generally less likely to take each other for granted. To approximate the old adage "distance makes the heart grow fonder," couples that live apart can acquire a deep appreciation for each other.

Traditionally, the alternative to the long-distance relationship has been for the woman to give up her career. Just the fact that this is no longer a given often makes for a better overall relationship. However, communication in a long-distance relationship does get tricky. Some couples correspond a great deal, talk on the telephone frequently, keep each other posted by sending cassettes through the mail, and work out both a schedule and a means to see each other whenever possible. Often, higher levels of passion result from the precious time together and make up for the missing element of comfort that characterizes these relationships.

A word of caution. Long-distance relationships usually go through an unexpected adjustment crisis when they cease to be long-distance. In many respects this is understandable. For one thing, one partner may have to give up career prospects to join the other; as a result, he or she has the triple stress of changing jobs while changing location *and* also redefining a relationship. And as one might expect, the new condition of living together on a daily basis necessitates a readjustment to each other's patterns. Close communication of the kind I described earlier is *essential* for long-distance couples who go through this transition.

PRIVACY

Each of us needs varying degrees of privacy—another matter that needs to be negotiated. The sooner in your relationship you define what's "yours" and negotiate what's "shared," the better for both of you. By privacy, I mean both physical privacy and emotional "space"—which could mean a "room of one's own" and the opportunity to enjoy solitude when you want it.

A common misconception says that privacy is needed only when there is something to hide. This is not true. A relationship where either person has to fight for his or her privacy can soon be in a lot of trouble. Generally it is the partner who has *less* of a need for privacy who feels threatened by the other person's need for time to himself or herself. If you are the one who has a greater need for privacy, you may need to provide reassurance that you are not shutting your partner out or rejecting that person in any way. If there is a difference in your attitudes toward privacy, it's also important for you to understand what your partner *does* like to share with you or others. Listening to each other and defining the differences in your attitudes may be a very important step.

Any relationship can seem strong if there are no stresses put on it, but each time an issue or crisis comes up and is successfully worked through, your relationship will become even stronger. On the other hand, when stress is at its lowest level, the patterns of communicating, resolving minor issues, and enjoying your privacy may still need attention. If you and your partner begin to see yourselves as people who can overcome many obstacles and survive numerous kinds of stresses and strains, you are truly building muscle in your relationship.

SUPPORTING YOUR PARTNER

What kind of support do you prefer from your partner when you are feeling needy or in crisis? For each person support has a different meaning. And knowing what your partner expects is crucial to knowing *who* your partner is as a person.

Unfortunately, we often give the type of support that helps *us* the most, rather than making the effort to see what kind of support *our partner* responds to the best. (Isn't this reminiscent of sexual preference and desire?) Having given that kind of support with the best intentions, you may find that it either doesn't work—or, worse yet, runs counter to what your partner really wants. When the two of you are caught in this bind, your partner may end up feeling negated, while you feel unappreciated. Nobody wins!

Some people prefer to be left alone during times of stress. If this is your preference, you may believe that leaving your partner alone is the best way to be supportive. But what if your partner prefers instead to have someone close to talk things over with. What if your partner wants someone just to listen? Or does your partner need someone who will provide physical comfort without being overly responsive verbally?

Everyone defines support in his or her own way when feeling needy, troubled, or in crisis. What do you prefer? What does your partner prefer?

Here are some common ways people define support from their partners. Neither is better or worse than any other, for each is a matter of taste.

• *Being left alone.* I put this one first because this is how in my relationship I prefer to be supported when I feel overwhelmed. It is important that I have at least a half hour or so to sort things out and then have the option of talking things over with my partner when I have gotten all I need out of my own solitude.

• *Holding and comforting.* Some people like not to talk but just to be soothed on a feeling level, or to be listened to without response.

• *Having the other person take over the situation.* Looking to one's partner to talk things over, to fact find, and possibly to act as the devil's advocate works for many.

Some people prefer different things at different times. Most importantly, when one of you is in crisis:

• Talk about how you feel when you're ready—*or ask for what you want.* Don't assume that your partner should know. Remember that sometimes we all have mixed feelings when we are feeling troubled. But as in all areas of your relationship, communicating with your partner will make a crucial difference. Remember, it's perfectly fine to be confused. You might say, "I'm so upset right now, I just can't sort out how I feel." Or, "I might want you to help me—but I don't know what I need yet." That's especially important if you just need time to sort things out.

• *Don't misinterpret your partner's request to be left alone as an attempt to shut you out.* This may merely be your partner's best way of dealing with the situation. If you are willing to step back when your partner needs some space, this is respectful of your partner's needs. On the other hand, if you feel threatened by being "shut out," you may be misinterpreting a short-term request for solitude as a way to "shut you out." In all likelihood, it's not that at all—and you'll be close as ever if you can just give your partner some space.

• *Don't be judgmental of your partner's preferences.* Preferences are not wisely judged as better or worse. We become the people we are through trial and error. Most of us develop our preferences because we find what really works for us, and we make choices for our own reasons, in our own ways.

MASTERING THE ART OF COMMUNICATION

Almost always, two people can learn how to communicate well if only they want to. This makes having comfort in your relationship something that is truly within your reach. By keeping the following additional points in mind, you and your partner together may be able to weather almost any issue or crisis.

• *Never negotiate when angry.* If there is an ongoing issue that is likely to come up, try to negotiate a win-win solution when you are feeling *good* about yourselves. Try to *initiate* negotiation by asking your partner to discuss an issue—with the understanding that this will infinitely help the relationship in the long run. Make sure that each of you has considered the other's perspective. If your partner is venting anger, sometimes it's better if you just back off. A full-blown argument (which nobody wins) cannot happen unless *both* of you collaborate.

• *Learn to empathize with your partner.* Empathizing does not necessarily mean agreeing, but simply understanding how your partner feels. Healthy relationships have plenty of space for disagreement, but much less room for lack of empathy. Be careful about what you share with your family and friends concerning your partner. Although discussing your relationship and its issues with outsiders may feel very good when you're angry, you will often regret it later on, after things get patched up.

• *Learn to take risks.* Never underestimate the power of risk-taking. Is there some issue that might be bothering your partner? Or an issue that has been bothering you, though you're reluctant to bring it up? A part of risk-taking is making your needs known—in fact, being vulnerable. Each time you open that channel of communication, it starts the momentum in a positive direction. Ultimately, taking those risks will make your relationship deeper, closer, and more enjoyable for both of you.

• *Practice what can be considered megacommunication, or communicating about your communication.* In other words, practice the kinds of listening exercises I described earlier. From time to time, check with each other to find out if there is anything that seems to be creating any negative residue. Set time aside to talk, turn off the TV, and remove any other distractions, even if it's just for ten or fifteen minutes. (I have yet to meet a couple who couldn't do this if they really tried.) Some of the most destructive issues in relationships build up slowly because they're not talked about. However, doing this *too* often can sometimes be destructive also.

• *No one has 100 percent of their needs fulfilled all the time.* Don't put negative labels on your relationship because it is sometimes unfulfilling. Accept that it simply *will* be unfulfilling at times. The fact that there are low lows in your relationship as well as some very good high points is just an indication that you're both human.

• *Work at achieving a balance together.* Avoid making one partner top dog and the other an underdog. When you and your partner have disagreements in such areas as whether to spend money, have sex, go on vacation, or have a child, usually the one who says no wins the argument. But when one person practically always says no, the relationship may be headed for trouble. It's fine to say no sometimes—but relationships that work best require a fair degree of compromise.

• *Put some humor into your interactions.* Learn to laugh at your issues. It's easier and more fun if you can loosen up together! Not only that, but humor is creative, because it turns "logic" upside down. You may find some imaginative ways to solve problems that have you stumped.

• *Once you've resolved an issue, let go of it.* Some couples find it helpful to establish a twenty-four- or forty-eight-hour rule. If it's not resolved within that period of time, it's dead forever. Don't dig up old "resolved" matters to justify your current argument. Look at it this way: If you're together twenty or fifty years, think of how much you could "have" on each other. Yes, if you wanted to let fly with a list of past misdeeds, you probably could. But there's no "win" in doing that.

Successful couples are those that *let go* of their anger and allow healing to occur.

Much of what was discussed in this chapter has been the aspects of communication that most couples learn to master, in their own ways, as they build a long-term relationship. If you can overcome communication barriers and work toward hearing and understanding each other, I believe that your relationship will stand an extremely good chance of weathering many storms. If not, there's a chance that things will go awry.

In the next few chapters, we'll look at some of the ways this can happen—and I'll recommend techniques that will help you and your partner deal with the more problematic issues that can arise when things do get out of hand.

PART TWO

Relationships in Trouble

CHAPTER FIVE

STORMY RELATIONSHIPS

Stormy relationships are usually characterized by an abundance—perhaps an overabundance—of passion, with less than enough comfort to provide balance. Whoever coined the adage "the honey is sweet, but the bee has a sting" had a stormy relationship in mind. If that applies to your relationship, then this is your chapter!

Most stormy relationships are usually characterized by anger, resentment, and extreme jealousy—that is, the brand of passion that builds into a negative force. In some relationships that's all there is. While in others, love and hate can coexist to such a degree that it can preoccupy either or both partners so much that it becomes more of an obsession.

Sheila and Troy, both young professionals in their late twenties, "fell in love" on their first date. Before the end of their first evening together, they actually agreed that they would marry. The wedding took place after a three-month whirlwind courtship, the likes of which neither of them had ever experienced. It was a second marriage for Sheila and the third for Troy. Each of them felt that their relationship was sealed by a degree of solid passion that exceeded all bounds.

Eight months later, they were separated. When they began therapy, both alluded to something that they felt they were missing. Sheila described that missing element as the "quietly boring" times she'd had in her first marriage. Troy talked about "constant demands"—and said he missed having "unpressured time." Unable to live a peaceful, comfortable, day-to-day coexistence, they often fought as passionately as they made love. As time went on, each found a great deal of fault with the other. Yet they couldn't "let go": Whenever they talked about going their separate ways, they would reconcile long enough for temporary forgiveness, passionate lovemaking, and heartfelt vows to try again. "This time we'll make it work," they declared repeatedly. Sheila described her marriage this way:

> I feel like I'm at my best and worst when I'm with Troy. I tolerate more from him than I ever have from anyone else. Yet, he can be very uncaring. Whenever I talk about our marriage to anyone else, I have a terrible time explaining why we stay together. In my heart of hearts, breaking up is out of the question. But I don't see how we're going to make it. I can't keep going through this.

This is how Troy described his marriage to Sheila:

> We never had much in common. We are of different religions; we don't like to spend our time doing the same things; and it seems as though Sheila blames me for everything that goes wrong in her life. When we argue, it's as if we hate each other, and we never seem to resolve anything. I thought I had the strength to do *anything*. But I can't seem to walk away— even though that's often what I want to do.

The chemistry between Sheila and Troy was so strong that it never occurred to them on the first date that they would have to work out many issues before even considering a commitment such as marriage. Once it became apparent that passion alone could not sustain the relationship, each blamed the other. Almost no area of comfort existed for them. Every disagreement became a life-and-death issue. For Sheila and Troy, the answer was to actually *decrease* their passion somewhat.

> ## REASONS YOUR RELATIONSHIP MAY BE STORMY

Stormy relationships have many possible causes. In some instances, one partner is usually the storm cloud—the other catches the lightning. In other relationships, the blowups are collaborations. However the storms occur, *they're never just one person's problem*. Stormy relationships just about always require two to tango.

To the extent that you are in a relationship that is characterized by storminess, see how many of the following apply to your situation.

• *You or your partner love each other—but you don't respect each other.* This means that you and your partner are capable of making each other *feel* very good at times, but when those good feelings go away (and all feelings and emotions by definition are temporary), either or both of you are left feeling a chronic void. And each of you blames the other for creating that feeling of emptiness.

• *Someone has low (or no) tolerance for frustration.* One or both of you find frustration so difficult to handle that you overreact. If you typically have difficulty with frustration and discomfort in other areas of your life, such as in dealing with other people, the same is probably true when you are in even the slightest conflict with your partner.

• *You project the things you like the least about yourself onto your partner.* When this happens, lack of tolerance for your own shortcomings gets converted into anger that's directed at your partner. In reality, this anger at yourself is fueled by low self-esteem.

• *You believe that virtually everything must be shared.* Some of the stormiest relationships are actually some of the most open ones. Under the banner of openness, one or both of you may feel that it is perfectly fine to exploit the vulnerabilities of the other. For example, if your partner is clearly wounded whenever you are attracted to a member of the opposite sex, you still feel a need to "share your feeling" with your partner. If that sexual attraction to someone else is trivial to you, then your "openness" is actually gratuitous.

• *You feel unlovable.* If this is the case, you may then escalate any disagreement with your partner into a feeling of being rejected as a person. The "issue" is forgotten; because that "unloved" feeling becomes uppermost.

• *One of you seeks to control the other.* Some couples manage to destroy the good things they have going for them by not dealing with their "control" issues head on. Especially today, relationships that fail are often the result of one partner trying to play a domineering, controlling role.

• *Displacement of anger.* When anger meant for someone else is repeatedly directed toward your partner, your relationship is probably headed for trouble. For instance, you might attack your partner with anger that is really meant for your boss, or with anger at a chronically frustrating situation at work. An example would also be anger at your parent of the opposite sex that gets acted out by attacking your partner as though he or she were that parent.

• *Winning your partner back becomes a game.* Some couples find that fighting and then making up, as a pattern, often leads to their best sex. A couple recently told me "after a fight is the time when we feel the most romantic." Is it any wonder that this couple fights a lot? Yet, what they really wanted were fewer fights and great sex. (For them the key was recognizing that the pattern had to be broken if their fights were to diminish. Could they find ways to have passionate sex *without* passionate fighting?)

• *Lack of communication about intimacy.* You or your partner cannot tolerate the same amount of intimacy on a consistent basis. You expect it to be more consistent than it is, or the two of you differ as to just how much closeness is optimal. Thus, one of you pulls away. The other then feels rejected. The partner pulling away meant no rejection, but failed to communicate that.

• *Both of you are too dependent.* If you or your partner feel that you have to count on the other person to support feelings of happiness and well-being, you blame the other when you begin to feel your own personal feelings of inadequacy.

• *One or both of you is the product of poor relationship modeling.* Perhaps the only way you ever learned how to resolve conflict was by observing your parents. But what if they were inadequate in this area? For example, if one parent left the house whenever there was an argument or conflict, perhaps you follow the same pattern. Or if they simply ignored each other, you may still operate from the assumption that people solve their problems by ignoring their spouses. But, remember, even if your parents stayed together, their system could spell the end of *your* relationship.

• *An ongoing issue lurks beneath the surface.* If a subject is taboo, you can be sure neither of you will be able to work it through. An example might be an affair that took place long ago. Perhaps it became taboo because you couldn't resolve the issue when you did try. But if that issue hangs on, it could produce a chronic negative feeling for your partner. Such feelings may range from occasional dislike to pure, consistent hatred. When couples are in this situation, and denying the issue, the charade leads you to displace your anger inappropriately onto lesser issues.

• *Unrealistic expectations of a relationship.* If you're constantly comparing your partner to some ideal, you can be sure your partner will never be just plain "good enough." If this is the case, you may want to look again at the discussion of unrealistic expectations in Chapter 1.

• *Chemical dependency.* If either or both of you abuse alcohol or drugs—and attempt to interact while under the influence— you are almost certain to be unable to resolve issues or have a fulfilling relationship.

• *One or both of you feel trapped.* Some couples stay together out of a fear of being lonely, a fear of risk and change, or an inability to believe that each of you can fare well enough on your own. Sometimes this occurs simply because one or both partners is too depressed to take the action that needs to be taken to end a relationship that must end. The issues of whether your relationship can be saved and how to get out of it if it can't will be addressed in Chapters 8 and 13, respectively.

Why do strong relationships remain that way? Why do partners remain "locked" in such relationships? Obviously, the reasons are many. But it helps to recognize what may be your blind spots. If you can recognize a pattern of interaction that creates "storms," that recognition can be the first and most difficult step toward turning things around.

TYPES OF STORMY RELATIONSHIPS

Relationships that bristle with negative passion often lead to extreme consequences. And many (if not most) stormy relationships do ultimately end. But ending a relationship is often needless, if only you are both willing to look at your patterns and to commit yourselves to changing them. How can extremely stormy relationships be changed in such a way that the partners can resolve some of their conflicts? Let's look at some specific situations.

ON AGAIN/OFF AGAIN RELATIONSHIPS

Gloria and Bill came in for couples counseling, after "ending" their five-year relationship for the ninth time. Theirs was the very definition of an on again/off again relationship. They had dated for a year; then after breaking up and reuniting several times, they decided that their problems would be over if Gloria moved out of her parents' home and moved in with Bill.

During the first year, however, Gloria moved back to her parents' home on three different occasions—lock, stock and barrel—only to return to Bill after they promised each other, "It will never happen again." The nature of the issues that drove them apart hardly mattered. When they disagreed about *anything*, they usually handled their differences in one of two ways. Either they "dropped" the subject without resolution, or they flew into an argument.

Arguments, for Gloria and Bill, were vicious matters. They pulled out all of the stops. They would get extremely personal, attacking everything from one another's families to sexual abilities. They resurrected old arguments and literally entered a contest to see who could best overwhelm and devastate their partner. As a consequence, nobody won any argument. They simply split up.

After one of their reconciliations, they decided that things would be better if they got married. So they did—and, for the next three years, incurred massive legal fees during their temporary separations. (Each time, one or the other resolved that this would be it—divorce was the only solution.) The money spent on all those collective legal fees topped the couple's annual joint income!

In order to break this on again/off again pattern, Gloria and Bill needed to learn how to fight fairly. Gloria, as it happened, came from a home where her mother had reigned supreme. She described her father as "a great guy, but henpecked." Bill's parents had been divorced when he was an adolescent. In his house, fighting had been continuous and unrelenting during the last three years that his parents had been together. Often, Bill's parents went for weeks without talking to each other.

When I brought up the idea of fair fighting, Gloria and Bill both looked at me as though I had spouted an oxymoron. However, by applying some fair fighting principles (which I'll discuss later in this chapter), they discovered that they could stay together, even if that meant staying uncomfortably together for awhile. They were able to recognize their pattern and, more importantly, they were able to look at some of their ongoing issues. Eventually, they learned some ways to reach resolutions without allowing their trademark anger to take over.

On again/off again relationships can have many go-arounds. But the pattern will ultimately end when each partner makes a commitment to:

- Not let each issue get out hand
- Learn fair fighting and basic communication skills
- Resist the urge to repeat their habitual pattern of breaking up—even if coexistence gets extremely uncomfortable for a period of time
- Use their brains as well as their feelings when resolving an issue

ABUSIVE RELATIONSHIPS

Abusive relationships rarely have a chance of working in the long run for anyone, unless the abuser sincerely recognizes the *form* of abuse and admits to committing it. Once the abuser takes that step, an ironclad agreement is necessary for both partners—together and separately—to do whatever needs to be done to end the abuse.

Amy and Sam had frequent arguments during their eighteen-year marriage. On numerous occasions, Sam would physically abuse Amy. When this happened, Amy often withdrew and became compliant on the outside, while seething with rage on the inside. She hoped that her "compliance" would make their situation at home more bearable.

Finally, Amy made arrangements to move with her two teenage children into a summer home owned by her parents. It was the first time in their marriage that they had been separated. Sam got the message and finally agreed to come into counseling.

"I must be a masochist or something to have put up with this kind of treatment for so long," Amy said during her first session.

I quickly pointed out that, if anything, she was quite the opposite of a masochist. A masochist is one who likes pain. Amy, on the other hand, didn't want to experience the pain connected with leaving the relationship; to avoid that pain, she put up with what she described as "the lesser pain of the abuse," while trying to protect her children and hold the marriage together.

On the surface, someone who stays in an abusive relationship may look foolish. But it is not quite that simple. This was especially so in the case of Amy and Sam. They had been through quite a bit together. Both had drinking problems in the early days of their marriage. Amy had almost given up drinking, and she was able to restrict herself to a modest amount on social occasions. Sam, on the other hand, was an alcoholic who attributed much of his behavior to his drinking. However, at the time I met them, he had been sober for about eight years; yet the abusive behavior has not changed that noticeably. Sam used the label "dry alcoholic" to describe himself.

The counseling began about a month after Amy had left Sam. I could see that there was a great deal of caring for each other, despite the weight of unresolved issues that had built up over the years. In counseling, Amy and Sam began to identify the early signs or warning signals that usually indicated that their arguing would get out of hand. Although Amy and Sam have not yet gotten back together, they have agreed that if they reconcile, and the pattern once again begins, that their next breakup will be a permanent one.

In an abusive relationship, it's essential to recognize the "warning signals"—as Amy and Sam learned to do—and to find ways in which to "de-escalate" the situation. To do that, it's usually necessary for both to recognize what makes a partner abusive. In broad terms, there are two types of abusive partners.

• *The abuser simply believes that it is okay to behave in an abusing manner.* In such cases, there is very little hope that there will be any change. Partners who are physically abusive without seeing their behavior as flawed will, predictably, keep on abusing. In extreme cases, the abuse may continue until tragedy ensues.

• *The abuser sees his or her behavior as a fault that needs to be corrected.* In such cases, abuse is usually the result of extremely low (or no) frustration tolerance and social conditioning. For instance, Sam's father was abusive to his mother; growing up, Sam was more or less conditioned to believe that this was the way a man solved arguments with his wife. The good news is that an abuser of this type will usually be willing to alter those destructive patterns. To the extent that the partner is intent on changing, the relationship becomes potentially salvageable. The more the abuser is truly upset with his or her own behavior (and not just opposed to the partner's reaction or threats to leave), the better the prognosis for change.

Of course, these two kinds of abusers often cannot be clearly labeled—and, in fact, those who abuse their partners usually are somewhere along the continuum between these two extremes. But for the other partner (the abused one) to make critical decisions about his or her future and safety, it's essential to recognize whether the abuser really wants to change or not.

If you are involved with a physically abusive partner, only you can decide how much you are willing to take before you end the relationship. Abusers are often sorry after the fact, and promise never to do it again. But because there are many complex reasons why people act out anger in this way, permanent change is sometimes a pipedream, and, nearly always, extremely difficult. In many cases, the abused partner slowly starts to develop a negative self-image that says, in essence, "I deserve this" or "I am inadequate to make it on my own." The abusing partner may consider the spouse as a possession and only seem affected when the abused is about to leave. The outburst of rage may trigger some romantic feelings; then both partners become passionate for a while until the crisis blows over. If this is the case, it is predictable that the abuse will continue.

The only way repeated abuse will be resolved permanently is for the abusing partner to halt the pattern before abuse occurs again. It is not within the abused partner's power to cure the abuse on his or her own. Often the problem is drug- or alcohol-related. But just as often it is merely a matter of low frustration tolerance, immaturity, and a sense of righteousness in the relationship. Probably that righteousness is a staple in other areas of his or her life as well.

In one survey, at least 1.8 million American women are severely beaten in their homes every year. This is a very underreported problem—much like rape—so that figure was probably underestimated. But it is also estimated that violence occurs at least once in as many as two-thirds of all marriages. Many women report being abused on a weekly basis, and/or sustaining serious physical injuries—not to mention the emotional ones. A violent death of either the abused partner or abuser (when the abused is pushed to the limit) is not uncommon.

Mental or emotional abuse is even more common. Either partner is just as likely to be the culprit here. Mental abuse happens when a partner expresses his or her rage viciously and excessively. Often, just as blatantly, there is a refusal to spend time working things out. Perhaps he or she refuses to do anything to make the relationship more bearable, is by all definitions uncaring, and is concerned only with his or her own needs. If this situation characterizes your relationship, I direct you to Chapter 8, which can help you to determine whether your relationship can be saved.

ADDICTIVE RELATIONSHIPS

Many people talk about "being trapped in a bad relationship." Some achieve what I have long called *a comfortable state of discomfort*. It seems logical to ask, if a situation is that bad, why not get out?

One reason, however, is that the situation isn't always "that bad." Often it only feels that way. Usually people are not actually trapped in a relationship; they only *feel* trapped. And there is an important distinction to be made. Though it is certainly possible that the relationship feels restricting to one or both partners, it's possible that it would feel *less* restricting if you changed some patterns that characterize your negative interaction.

Believe it or not, we have learned a lot over the years about addictive relationships through experiments with rats and other animals. Extreme anxiety can be induced by confusing pleasure and pain. In one classical experiment, a dog was shown a straight line that represented pain (by getting an electrical shock) and a circle that represented reward (by getting a food treat). Each time the dog was shown the line, it would recoil in anticipation of pain. When shown the circle it would salivate, a reaction representing pleasure. Slowly the line became less straight and more circular, and the circle would become more oblong. As soon as the dog could not distinguish between the two, there was an extreme amount of confusion and panic. This is called an experimentally induced neurosis.

What is significant to us is that many relationships operate under the same principle, where the pain that characterizes a relationship as well as the pleasure get dealt out in very unpredictable doses. As soon as one cannot distinguish whether pain or pleasure will be coming, all perspective can become lost. This can cause a collapse in communication and make every other aspect of the relationship, even the positive ones, seem out of reach.

The principle applies even in a relationship that is characterized by an *extreme* amount of pain. As long as there is some pleasure, comfort, or security, two people can stay emotionally hooked to each other for an indefinite period of time. What I have described is the essence of an addictive relationship. Later on in the book we will talk about how one can break free, if this is your choice. But for now, let's assume that your choice is to resolve the pain by changing those patterns that characterize your negative interaction.

FIGHTING FAIRLY

If you would describe your relationship as "stormy," no matter what the specific issues, it will be essential for you and your partner to learn to fight fairly.

Let's face it, practically all couples argue. But if you characterize your relationship as stormy, chances are that you and your partner allow your arguments to escalate. Sometimes, just about every issue that comes up results in an argument. Then the argument takes on a life of its own, and you both get hooked.

Before looking at some very specific dos and don'ts, consider the following possible outcomes of any conflict you may be having.

• *A lose/lose solution.* This is where each person comes out of the conflict without achieving his or her goal. Sometimes a lose/lose situation occurs when one partner or the other wins a concession, but then loses on the more intangible or long-term level of the relationship.

• *Win/lose solution.* This describes a situation where in order for one partner to get his or her way the other partner must *not*—by definition—get his or her way. The trick then becomes to see which partner can overpower the other, and the game becomes control. This often works in business, but rarely in relationships.

• *Win/win solution.* In this outcome, both people get something of what they want. Thus, neither feels used or exploited. Win/win solutions usually come as the result of each partner making some sort of compromise. That means neither may get everything he or she wants, but each gets enough to come out of the conflict with dignity, and maybe even with positive feelings intact. This is the most rational goal to keep in mind whenever conflict resolution is called for. To achieve a win/win solution, consider these "dos and don'ts" as guidelines.

DON'TS

• *Don't displace anger.* Make sure you are discussing the issue you mean to be discussing, and with the person you need to be discussing it with. Don't ventilate anger that belongs elsewhere toward your partner!

• *Don't air dirty laundry.* It is usually best to keep arguments private and to avoid embarrassing each other by arguing and fighting in public or in front of family or friends.

• *Don't think about winning or losing.* Instead, concentrate on resolving the problem. Remember, if both of you are concentrating on winning, at least one of you will lose in the short run. Thus, no one will ultimately win, which means both of you will probably lose.

• *Don't keep things pent up* to the point where your fight will become an overreaction to the issue at hand. Work to keep current with your feelings.

• *Don't be archeologists.* Avoid digging up old material that is no longer relevant.

• *Don't be afraid to back off sometimes.* Not every issue is that important to both of you. Good relationships are ones in which neither of you is afraid to be flexible, to compromise, and to give in when appropriate.

• *Don't let things get out of hand.* If you lose your focus, one of you should blow the whistle and stop the discussion. Many couples find that by actually having a code word for stopping a fight that's going nowhere, the issue can often be resolved with much less pain.

• *Don't overreact to your partner's anger.* This will only continue the vicious circle. Sometimes by merely letting your partner ventilate, the anger will soon be gone and then you can *discuss* the issue.

• *Don't threaten or talk about divorce* or separation in the middle of an argument.

• *Don't leave the house in the middle of an argument.* It is okay and even admirable to back off (and backing off is not leaving). But relationships are one instance where you can run but you can't hide.

• *Don't open a Pandora's box* on every (or, better yet, any) issue.

DOS

• *Do fight with your head*—not strictly with your emotions. Your emotions may be what got you into the conflict, but it's your head that will find you that win/win solution.

• *Do take responsibility for your own feelings.* Keep other people's opinions, and things other people may have said, out of the argument. Try to avoid acting like a prosecutor—looking for more and more evidence to indict your partner.

• *Do listen to your partner.* Before you react to your partner's words, listen to them. He or she may actually have a point! Whether or not you will ultimately agree with it, at least *know* your partner's point of view.

• *Do fight clean.* That means without bringing to the discussion sensitive issues that have no relevance. Forget the martyr stuff such as, "Look at all I've done for you" and "If you really love me you would . . ."

ONGOING STICKY ISSUES

Sometimes an issue in your relationship can resemble a stubbed toe. You can be perfectly healthy, but by stubbing a tiny toe, you can be in such excruciating pain that you wish you were dead! Many relationships have an ongoing sticky issue like this. If yours has one that doesn't seem to go away (and indeed some relationships have issues that have been present for many decades!), at sometime other than during an intense battle about it between the two of you, try to establish a procedure to deal with it. Most couples fail to take this step. The result could be that you wind up with a situation that remains the same indefinitely or even worsens. Examples of sticky issues include:

• Problems with in-laws, relatives, or certain friends outside the relationship
• Disagreements about the children
• Disagreements over career or work issues
• Certain decisions that always seem to favor one person in the relationship
• Sex (or the lack thereof), including disagreements about the type and frequency of sex
• Issues about former lovers and other matters that lead to jealousy

- Issues about how your time is spent together or apart
- Areas of special sensitivity that are sure to trigger hurt in you or your partner

Obviously, the best way to handle a sticky issue is to nip it in the bud as soon as possible—early in the relationship—or as soon as it begins to become a problem for either of you. However, often this is easier said than done. But whether this has been your Achilles heel for decades or you are just beginning, try this procedure:

- *Step One.* Take time when you are *feeling good* about yourself and each other. Sit down and negotiate a procedure for handling your problem the next time it comes up.
- *Step Two.* It is most important that when you are negotiating *procedure* that you avoid getting into an argument about the situation or problem itself at this time, or you will be likely to induce the battle that you are trying to avoid.
- *Step Three.* Put your procedure *in writing*. Each of you should sign it and keep a copy handy. Make your written procedure as detailed as possible, taking into consideration practically anything that can go wrong in using it. Be as creative as you can about your procedure; it can take many forms. The most important thing is that your procedure be spelled out as something that can be easily followed. Even more importantly, make it something you are going to stick to, so that your argument can end in the shortest possible time.
- *Step Four.* When the issue comes up next, the person *not yet as angry* will refer to this agreement that you set up and follow the detailed step by step procedure spelled out. This may even include the more angry person (or each of you separately) ventilating, without retaliation until the argument loses steam.

Ironically, once the procedure is developed, the issue (as a by-product) sometimes resolves as well. But this is not always the case. Most couples have something that one or both partners blow out of proportion. This is what triggers the tendency to become irrational. Resolving it rarely happens unless the two of you can agree you have a problem. But if you can, that in and of itself is often much more than half of the battle.

HOW TO BUILD UP YOUR COMFORT LEVEL WITHOUT LOSING THAT POSITIVE PASSION

Changing destructive patterns in your relationship—no matter how long they have been going on—is a task that I believe is within the grasp of practically every couple. The only requirement is that both of you become committed to making your relationship a less stormy one. But the key word here is *both*. Just as you have each played a part in getting into a destructive pattern together, you will need to collaborate equally to abolish the pattern.

Think of a stormy relationship as being a circular pattern. In all probability, each of you is doing your part to trigger negative responses in the other. These responses may be inappropriate. Nevertheless, they become predictable habits.

Usually, when a couple is locked in a stormy relationship, both are unhappy, and the unhappiness causes pain. So it's in both your interests to break the pattern. Here are some suggestions that have helped many couples to do that:

• To help restore sorely needed comfort to your relationship, try to agree that neither of you will leave the relationship at the next crisis—even if it becomes quite uncomfortable for a time. If you can agree on this point, it takes away one of the big escalating factors—the recurrent threat to "walk out" on the other person. For example, when Amy and Sam used to fight, arguments always escalated into a question of who would leave the other first. They couldn't argue about an issue without trying to wound each other by threatening to leave. Once they agreed that they would both stay through the next crisis—despite the discomfort—it became essential for them to find a *means* of resolving their disputes rather than walking away from them.

• I often suggest to couples that as early as possible they draw up what I lightheartedly refer to as a *psychological prenuptial agreement.* Just as people who are getting married or entering into live-in arrangements draw up legal prenuptial agreements to deal with property and other legal issues should the marriage get out of hand, a psychological prenuptial agreement can be helpful as well.

This can help you to determine how you will deal with various issues that you may encounter at times of stress—when you may be less capable of handling them. The idea is to anticipate issues that you think you *may have* difficulty with, to work out solutions *before* emotions begin clouding things over. It is easier to resolve a potential problem than one that has become full-blown.

• *It is perfectly okay for the two of you to agree that certain topics are taboo.* For example, many couples find that talking about things such as previous lovers or past romances will pull the scab off whatever healing has occurred. If you have items that fit into this category—and you know what they are—make an ironclad agreement to stay away from those topics. Then stick to that agreement.

• *Get into the habit of taking responsibility for your own feelings and not blaming your partner.* As one person said to me recently, "I feel like a TV set to which my partner has the remote control." Granted, it may sometimes feel that way, but the more you understand that it is *you and your own attitudes* that ultimately cause your emotions to develop, the less you will blame your partner, and the more you will become in control of your life in general.

• *While having petty arguments, try exaggerating both the problems and your feelings about those problems to the point of absurdity.* When you both agree that it is getting absurd and funny, you will feel a cloud lift, and there's a good chance you won't fight about that issue again. It is obviously the one who is the least angry who will be most capable of injecting lightness and humor into the interaction. However, it's also important to recognize when issues are too close to be taken lightly. In some instances your partner needs support until a mood lifts or a situation improves. But if the time is right, making fun of yourselves and your quirks can be not only healing but fun. Sometimes an important step is to agree with your partner that you will help each other to do this when appropriate. For example, one couple I know has found that if each of them mimicks the other's overly serious face, they can often short-cut escalating anger.

• *Don't use an argument as a test of love.* One of the most common problems in stormy relationships is that someone puts their love on the line for each issue. This is what's happening when someone says, "If you really loved me, you would . . ." Usually, the other person feels trapped by a test like that. Does someone always have to "give in" to prove that he or she loves the other person? Which brings up the next suggestion for fair fighting . . .

• *Avoid putting your partner in a double bind.* Some couples, for example, have an unspoken rule that during an argument the partner who backs down gets the blame for the issue. Make sure you don't work to perpetuate your anger by neither of you giving the other a way out.

• *Try to get to the real issue.* If you and your partner are constantly picking fights, especially about the same things while avoiding the underlying issue, *the issue you are avoiding will probably not go away.* And if you continue to avoid the *real* issue, you are probably just prolonging the pain.

While there are many ways to help resolve the issues in a stormy relationship, remember that you and your partner need to fight the *pattern* of your arguments rather than fight each other. And that means doing something different from what you've done before. For instance, if you each go to opposite ends of the house and slam doors, that's a pattern—but one or both of you has the power to break that pattern. And a start might be someone saying, "I don't want to slam doors this time. I want to know why you're angry. I want to tell you why I'm angry. I want to work this out."

Of course, *breaking* patterns takes practice too—especially if those patterns have built up during many repetitions. But to the extent that you both agree that you want more comfort and less pain in your relationship, breaking those old patterns *is possible.*

CHAPTER SIX

WHEN INDIFFERENCE PREVAILS

Relationships that are characterized by indifference are often the most difficult ones to save. By indifference I am referring to a chronic lack of passion. Partners are often cold and aloof with each other. They seem to be uncaring, unresponsive, and unemotional toward each other. Often, at least on the surface, they are unsympathetic.

Underneath that indifference, there may be rather intensely passionate feelings, either positive or negative. But in some cases the indifference may be all there is: The passion just isn't there. The reason indifferent relationships are so difficult to turn around is usually because there's a lack of motivation behind one or both partners to work toward making a change. However, when the indifference conceals passion—and deprives both partners of comfort—it may be quite possible for them to turn things around.

In Molly and Keith's relationship, I had observed all the signs of complete indifference. When they came into therapy, however, they truly wanted to identify "what was missing" and to change their relationship for the better.

Keith's job required that he be away during the week visiting various branches of his company around the country. Most weeks, he left their home on Sunday night and did not return until late Friday afternoon.

During weekends and the few weeks when he came home at night, he and Molly had what I would call a pseudorelationship. To all appearances, they were husband and wife, but they interacted as little as possible.

It had been at least two years since they had had sex. What conversations they had were focused almost exclusively on issues involving money, the children, and other practical matters. Reaching this arm's-length existence was not something that happened overnight. It was a slow, gradual, eroding process. However, both Keith and Molly agreed that the deterioration began when Keith was offered his current job, which involved a substantial promotion; Molly had vigorously opposed his taking the job, she liked to have her husband around most of the time. When Keith went ahead and accepted the job anyway, Molly turned deeply resentful. Keith, in turn, resented her refusal to support him in his career. Little by little they drifted further and further apart.

Neither of them liked to argue or to act maliciously toward each other. That wasn't their style of coping. They just simply "turned off." On the verge of separating, they had decided to enter counseling as a last resort.

Keith was forty-eight years old, Molly forty-five. Although Keith was achieving a great deal of success in his work, he felt quite unfulfilled as a person. Molly was dreading the next year when her youngest child would go away to college. "I never thought I would see the day when the only thing I looked forward to was to go to work in the morning," Molly said.

Keith talked about how he used to look forward to doing things around the house on weekends. But his interest in that had faded. "Sometimes I literally hate this house brick by brick," Keith said in quiet yet enraged resignation.

In counseling they admitted to each other that neither wanted to separate or divorce. At its best, their marriage had a great deal of comfort. They both described themselves and each other as good parents. And neither had an alternative that seemed better.

At its worst, however, the marriage spelled loneliness for both. They were at a genuine impasse, unable to provide relief for each other.

SIGNS OF INDIFFERENCE

Signs that your relationship is suffering from indifference are quite specific. Nevertheless, it is important to keep in mind that there are *degrees* of indifference. Practically every relationship will reflect some indifference sometimes. It might be helpful to look at some of the thoughts and feelings that characterize this kind of relationship. Do any of them apply to you?

• You discover you and your partner have no real interest in each other's activities.

• You feel lonelier when you are with your partner than when you are apart.

• You feel happy when you can get away from your partner for your own solitude, and you don't look forward spending time together.

• You characterize (perhaps only to yourself) your relationship and your partner as boring.

• The thought of your partner going away for a long period of time or taking the responsibility for the two of you to separate brings on a happy feeling.

• You think more about how others react to your relationship breaking up than how you or your partner would feel if that happened.

• You have a lack of sexual interest in each other.

• You feel more like roommates than lovers. As one couple once described it, "We have a grandparents' divorce," referring to the generation when the norm was not to separate or divorce but simply to become distant yet accepting of the situation. Each day you become more and more like two strangers living in the same house, and your emotional distance gets greater. (One couple described this as their relationship "being on an artificial respirator.")

• Although you are in fact involved, you have a difficult time explaining—even to yourself—what keeps you together, other than practical matters such as the children, money, or the fears related to separating or being alone.

• The pain that characterizes your feelings about the relationship is a pain of emptiness and depression, which causes you to experience a lack of motivation.

HOW DID WE EVER GET THIS WAY?

If these are among your feelings, it might be important to look objectively at the way your relationship evolved. You both may have developed indifference as a way of coping with difficult situations, or as a way of "getting through" very stressful times. Indifference *does* serve a purpose; sometimes it actually helps a relationship to develop or survive.

A number of factors may cause partners to be indifferent, even from the beginning of their relationship:

• Some relationships or marriages are more or less "arranged," that is, the partners came together not because they had a strong desire to be together but because of social conditioning. Believe it or not, this practice is still the norm in many countries and was even quite common in America until this century. Obviously, when a relationship begins on this footing, the partner's indifference is quite understandable.

• When two people initially become a couple out of some necessity, such as an unwanted pregnancy or financial hardship, indifference may be the result. Once again, the partners were never really bonded to each other in the first place. That doesn't mean they can never become bonded, but in these cases breaking the aura of indifference is more of an uphill battle.

• Some relationships form because of social pressure. Partners become convinced by themselves or others that the next natural step in their relationship is to become a "permanent couple"—through marriage or some other form of commitment. In this relationship the two partners become a couple even though they are not really driven by much passion.

More commonly, however, relationships *become* indifferent. and this can be for a variety of reasons.

• *An unresolved issue breeds such resentment that there is a slow drifting apart.* Perhaps it is not the style of either partner to engage in anger-driven passion or any of the other kinds of behavior that characterize stormy relationships. When neither can express his or her feelings, a buildup of anger *slowly* undermines what passion was there. (One couple described their relationship as "quietly stormy.")

• *Partners grow in different directions.* Indifference then becomes the result of either not recognizing or not attending to the issues that come up as a result of their slow drifting apart.

• *A phenomenon occurs that is similar to the differences that couples have in their desire for sex or privacy.* In this case, the difference is in the amount of affection and intimacy. Sometimes, the partner with the greater need in the relationship believes that "You shouldn't have to ask for what you want." At some point, the partner desiring more may begin to feel rejected and start pulling away. There is a negative snowballing effect, as the other partner cannot interpret this pulling away. The "guessing game" becomes so complicated that basically both try to ignore each other. The result is indifference.

• *Broken trust or lack of respect* may result from some extremely difficult crisis, such as an affair by one partner. Partners become accustomed to an uncaring attitude where quiet hostility is the norm.

• *Couples who are afraid to express anger and other feelings keep them bottled up inside.* Holding back on negative feelings that need to be resolved often results in blocking positive feelings as well.

• *Either or both partners are suffering from depression or inhibited sexual desire.* This condition is assumed to be a sign that the relationship is burning out rather than being recognized as a symptom that can be treated. In this situation, a self-fulfilling prophecy is created: Indifference in the relationship makes sexual intimacy even more unlikely, if not impossible.

• *Some couples adopt a norm of maintaining the comfort they have in their relationship at all costs.* In an extreme case, there would be no fights, few (if any) minor disagreements, and little intimacy. Breaking that pattern is not seen as an option since it would involve risk. This is a common pattern for second marriages where one or both partners have bad memories of the storms of anger that "broke up" a first marriage. They want to avoid a repetition of that experience at all costs. Unfortunately, the cost can be greater distance in their current relationship, since issues are not openly addressed.

• *Indifference can be the result of any degree of abuse in a relationship.* Commonly, the abused partner builds a wall of protection against caring too much and becoming disappointed, hurt, or devastated once again.

• *Relationships that exploit one partner's vulnerabilities* also can create the necessity for that "wall" to protect you from getting hurt.

• *Drug and alcohol abuse* often siphons away passionate feelings and leaves indifferent ones in their place.

• *One (or both) partner(s) simply loses interest in the other.* Sometimes there's another person involved (with one or both partners), sometimes there isn't.

REVERSING THE TREND OF INDIFFERENCE

Although indifference can be a very difficult pattern to change in a relationship, it's certainly possible. If you feel there is a degree of indifference in your relationship, you can change that—either by rekindling what was once there or by creating a better climate in your relationship. In fact, you may be able to create a degree of comfort that you never had before, assuming that a change for the better is something that you both desire.

The first step in reversing your indifference is to recognize what caused it in the first place and to talk about how you can work together to come closer to each other.

Note that *someone* has to initiate this—and getting started is often the most difficult step. It might be as simple as saying, "I'm so unhappy about the lack of feeling that has come between us. I don't believe it always has to be this way." If your partner is equally unhappy and ready to address the issue, those words could be the most important ones you'll ever speak.

On the other hand, are you ready to be that vulnerable? Suppose your partner's indifference hides resentment or rage. He or she might respond, "I'm not being cold—you are." Or, "What's there to talk about?" Or even, "I don't see any change. We've always been this way."

It is important that both of you see how critical it is to start communicating. To do this, first identify those situations in the last section of this chapter that apply to your relationship. Start by discussing the trends you agree on. Next, you may find yourself directed back to the first four chapters in this book, especially Chapter 3 (Keeping Passion Alive) and Chapter 4 (Communication Styles). In addition to the suggestions in those chapters, consider the following points designed to zero in on your present predicament.

• Consciously begin to *concentrate on the things that you like most about your partner* instead of those things you dislike the most.

• *Try to find and identify the ingredients that brought you together in the first place.* Explore ways you can re-create the positive feelings you once had. Try to remember what made your partner so special initially. What did you do when you were dating, when you first began to live together? When did those nice things stop? Why? Chances are that in sharing some of these things that are important but rarely discussed, you will have surprises in store for one another.

• *Try to make it a rule that you won't "sweep things under the rug."* When new problems and issues come up, talk about them as soon as possible. Don't put them aside with the hope that they will simply go away. As you've probably learned, that hope is rarely fulfilled.

• *Make a list of those items that led to your indifferent feelings in the first place.* Become familiar enough with them that you can remind each other when one of you begins to repeat the pattern. For example, if you know you leave the room every time you're angry during an uncomfortable discussion, take responsibility for changing that pattern. Walk *back* to your partner and reopen the discussion—no matter how uncomfortable it feels. Changing the pattern is possible as long as at least one of you is willing to relentlessly pursue change.

• *Begin reestablishing intimacy* by sharing new feelings and information with your partner. Perhaps you felt your partner didn't care about this part of your life—or that you would be rejected if you shared certain thoughts and emotions. But if you begin this kind of openness, together you will start to bring that intimacy back once again. In other words, even if you feel as if you already know your partner, get to know each other again.

• *Take time to be together without other people around.* Many couples get into the habit of relaxing only when sharing activities as a family (that is, with children around) or when they are with other couples. As awkward as it may seem at first, *make being alone together* a top priority. Initially, you may have to be very deliberate about this—literally "making an appointment" to spend an evening together by yourselves or to take a weekend at the shore. But, eventually, it becomes comfortable and natural again.

• *Discuss what your goals together are*—both long- and short-term. There is a good chance that both of you have goals that have changed since the last time you discussed them. (Or perhaps you never discussed them.) You may find out some very valuable information about yourselves. And while you're at it, share the feelings that go along with wanting to achieve those goals—even if those feelings involve hoping, dreaming, and wishing.

• *Spend a week acting as if you were in love again.* Some couples do this by going away together or finding other ways to re-create their courtship. See how that feels and what it brings up for each of you.

• *If there is no motivation* to do any of these things, is it because you are afraid of being vulnerable? Do you want a non-relationship with the façade of a relationship? Are you really less unhappy (or more content) in your relationship than you may have previously thought you were? These are important questions to explore, and I'll have more to say about them later in the book.

• *Try reframing your problems.* Perhaps you have felt a lot of frustration recently due to missed expectations. Take the risk and turn to, instead of away from, your partner for support. You might begin by saying, "I've been very let down recently, because . . . I know you can't change that, but I'd like to tell you how I've been feeling."

• If you have been feeling the loneliness that many people in relationships *do* feel—yet believe they shouldn't—make a special effort not to blame your partner. Instead, look for the answer within yourself as to what it is you are really longing for. The answer may lie in disappointment at your own career development or in other issues outside the relationship. In this case, *your partner may have been an easy mark to blame for your own lack of fulfillment.*

It's also important to keep in mind that your partner can't always fix things for you when you are depressed or enraged at "the way things are going." Often, we secretly expect our partner to make up for what we feel we're missing. But no one can do that for us—so it's unrealistic to blame your partner. If your partner has taken blame for your own lack of ful-fillment in the past, try to keep that pattern from creeping in again. Your partner is not to blame—and, just as important, neither are you. The fact is, we all have some areas where we feel unfulfilled. Can you acknowledge that? If so, it's more likely that you will be able to have a better understanding of what your relationship *can* and *cannot* do for you.

For Molly and Keith it was this understanding that marked the beginning of their healing process. They are still together, and they describe their relationship as "off life supports" and working better than it has in a long time.

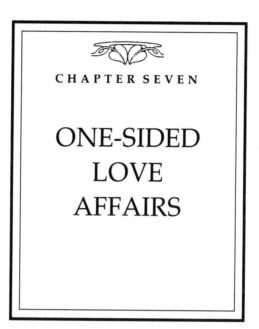

CHAPTER SEVEN

ONE-SIDED LOVE AFFAIRS

When your involvement is not mutual, the result can be pain for both people, but especially for the one who is more committed to the relationship. Unrequited love has indeed been known to trigger some of the most painful emotions. Sometimes just the recognition that your relationship comes under this category is all that is needed to help you make the necessary choices. For some that could even include staying in a relationship that many would define as "unworkable." For others, it means getting out. Unfortunately, too many choose the unworkable option of settling for no less than the change *in the other person* that will—at last—make involvement in their relationship mutual. But changing your partner's attitude toward you without his or her consent is generally impossible. And when you merely keep trying to change your partner, it's like banging your head against a brick wall.

It is that inability to make your partner feel something for you that he or she either chooses not to feel, or is unable to feel, that practically every one-sided love affair has in common. The big variable, of course, is how vested you are in the situation. Consider the following examples:

• Larry, an attorney, has a crush on a very attractive client who is married. Larry also describes himself as being happily married. Although he admits flirting sometimes, he does not expect his infatuation to go anywhere and describes the situation as benign.

• Tracey was involved for three years with a married man who says he loves her, yet refuses to leave his wife.

• Sue seems to practically "give her heart away" for the asking. She typically involves herself with men who show little interest in her other than what she can do for them. When she begins to act needy of more affection or commitment, they typically leave her.

• Kenneth and Sandy work together. They became friends around the time when Sandy's marriage was starting to break up. Sandy was in a lot of pain, and they slowly began what they each thought was a beautiful love affair. But after Sandy finally left her husband, her feelings for Kenneth cooled off considerably. For Kenneth, this was devastating.

• Tom and Nora always thought they had a very loving and supportive marriage. Nora always seemed to give Tom a great deal of support and mothering, yet asked for little in return. Then she found out she had breast cancer and for the first time in their ten-year marriage, she relied on Tom for support. Tom became distant and cold and even resentful that Nora was not as available to him as she had been in the past.

Some of these relationships were obviously one-sided from their inception, while others became that way during crises. In some cases, having unrequited feelings is quite harmless, while in others, the pain for either or both people can be excruciating.

CRUSHES

Larry had a crush on his client; and often, such crushes are destined to lead nowhere. But they can still be a great deal of fun. They can feel wonderful, and are harmless as long as they are kept on a fantasy level and the object of your crush is not someone with whom you become obsessed.

As we will see later in this book, very few people are completely exclusive with their partners, on a mental level. But when you are infatuated with someone, it is often the *role* of that person who is the object of your crush that is really what attracts you. This was the situation in Larry's case. All he needed to realize was that as long as he did not let the situation get out of hand by becoming especially solicitous to his client, no harm would be done.

I urge people who have this kind of harmless crush *not to feel guilty about it*, since it rarely has to have any implications whatsoever for your own real or primary relationship. Whether you try to take the matter any further is a choice only you can make based on your own values. Crushes can be a highly private and individual matter that need never become painful, unless you allow the situation to get out of hand. Remember, nowhere is it written that feelings must ever be acted upon, or even shared.

Of course, if you and the object of your affections are both available, and there are no other reasons to consider yourself or that other person an inappropriate partner, why not take the risk and explore the situation? Many great relationships have started out this way.

INVOLVEMENT WITH PEOPLE WHO ARE MARRIED OR OTHERWISE INVOLVED

Your deepest attractions may be toward those who are married or are otherwise involved. In fact, you may find that this kind of relationship works very well for you. Being involved with a married person is a way of having your cake and eating it too. You can have lots of passion, a surprisingly high level of comfort, and at the same time have little in the way of responsibility toward your partner.

The most difficult and painful aspect of involvement with someone who has another primary relationship occurs when it becomes your expectation to take over the role of that primary partner, and the object of your affections refuses or interminably delays leaving his or her spouse. Remember, *that seat is taken.* When this is the case, it usually follows that your partner's marriage or primary relationship will outlast the relationship you have together.

In addition, if your otherwise-involved partner is with someone else in a primary relationship, then at best yours is a secondary relationship. This means that you can practically count on him or her not being available to you at certain times when you are most in need. So, if it is a primary relationship you are looking for, and the person you are involved with is unable to make a firm commitment to end his or her primary involvement by a specified time, it is probably in your best interest to move on.

On the other hand, you may be a person who enjoys the brevity of encounters that you have with an otherwise involved partner. Maybe in your heart of hearts you really don't want a mutual primary relationship. If this is so, perhaps you are merely telling yourself at times that you *should* want it because that is the "correct" thing to want. Often this is a very tough thing to admit to yourself. But for many who get involved with one married lover after another, when these affairs do not mature into long-term relationships the result can be much unhappiness. Why? There might be a number of reasons:

• You may be telling yourself that all of the "good" men or women are married. To the extent that you firmly believe that, not only are you putting yourself down (because you aren't married), but it is very likely that your sensors are eliminating eligible members of the single population before you have really given them a chance. One woman recently told me while explaining why she had turned down a friend's offer to fix her up with an eligible single man: "If he was so great, he'd be married at thirty-seven."

• You could actually be longing for a more full-time primary relationship, though you really fear it. After all, if your involvement with someone who is committed elsewhere fails, you have a built-in excuse. Moreover, many find that involvement with married lovers provides protection from the issues of primary involvement. These issues might include:

  • Ambivalence about having children.
  • The experience of a painful divorce; perhaps you "will do anything" to avoid repeating that experience.
  • Getting over a previous involvement with someone who was overly demanding, needy, and who did not allow you enough privacy. Relationships with married people give you the opportunity to take regular breaks from each other. When he or she leaves to go home, your privacy is intact.

THE CASE FOR BEING INVOLVED WITH PEOPLE WHO ARE MARRIED OR WITH OTHER PRIMARY PARTNERS

Although I have known several single men who have been involved with married women, there are overwhelmingly more women involved with married (or otherwise "taken") men. And the women who discuss this issue with me generally describe some degree of criticism or ridicule that they get from family or friends. It's not surprising, therefore, that many automatically put themselves down as well.

However, what if you have chosen this kind of relationship because freedom is the most important thing to you? You are willing to concede (or even relish) the fact that most of the hours of the day will belong to your partner's other family obligations or be connected to his or her primary relationship.

When you actually "relish" such commitments, your partner's primary relationship is seen as an insurance policy guarding you against the possible loss of your freedom. Perhaps you like things exactly the way they are. In fact, if there are any fears at all, it is that the other person *will* leave his or her primary relationship for a more full-time involvement with you. If you have no intention of ending the relationship as long as it stays the way it is, but cringe at the thought of having to be the primary partner, then perhaps you have exactly what you want.

Mary had been dating a married man; and she found that she was sometimes criticized for it. Resolving her dilemma meant learning how to ignore what criticism she got and realizing that her arrangement did not conflict with her own value system.

> After having been in a marriage that made me constantly choose between my husband and my career, I have come to grips with the fact that I don't want to have children and I relish my freedom. Dating a married man, I have found, is the best of all possible worlds. I definitely have the passion I need from a man, yet I feel no obligation. If the right career opportunity came along, I could pick myself up and move to the opposite coast without feeling that anyone else even has to be consulted. It took me a long time to realize that I could have that kind of attitude, but in trying to do it the conventional way, I was never nearly as happy as I am now. At one time my family considered me cold and selfish for being able to think this way. But I can assure you that the man I am involved with would consider me anything but cold and selfish.

In the three-year period following Mary's divorce, she dated several men who were looking for primary relationships. When things got to the point where she began to feel responsible for providing the *quantity* of involvement they wanted, she began to lose interest. Mary doesn't close the door to ever entering into a primary relationship with someone who is totally available, but she emphatically states that when she does it will be because it feels right to her, not because it is "the right thing to do."

Lisa believes that she is just "plain not ready" to make a long-term commitment. Her views are similar to Mary's. Both Lisa and Mary agree that there are times when their partners are unavailable when they wish they could be with them. But as Lisa put it: "Do you know anyone who has everything they want?" That sounds like a question that could be asked of anyone at any level of involvement, conventional or otherwise.

In Chapter 10, we will explore triangles, parallel relationships, and the issues that the partner involved in another primary relationships faces, as well as other nonexclusive arrangements.

What is most important to realize about the type of secondary-primary arrangements I have described above is that they *can* work. I have seen some of them last for indefinite periods of time as long as both people have the same level of involvement in mind. As soon as that changes, however, it's usually only a matter of time before the relationship ends—sometimes with a great deal of pain, and often with devastating consequences.

Tracey, mentioned at the beginning of this chapter, was involved in a situation where she did want to be the primary partner; but the man she was involved with refused to leave his wife. When she finally realized how unlikely it was that her wish would ever be fulfilled, she painfully but decisively moved on. She is now involved with a man for whom she is the primary relationship; but to reach this point, she first had to give up the pipedream that her married partner would eventually leave his wife.

REBOUND/PREBOUND RELATIONSHIPS

Rebound and prebound relationships were discussed briefly in Chapter 1. Now I'd like to deal with each of these kinds of relationships in more depth. Both rebound and prebound relationships form frequent patterns of behavior in the lives of many people without their recognizing it. Probably the rebound relationship is the more well-known, so let's look at it first.

The rebound relationship is one in which the rebounder becomes emotionally involved too soon after the death of a previous partner or the breakup of a prior relationship. Often, it's hard for a rebounder to make the emotional commitment necessary for a new involvement that's satisfactory to both partners. Rebounders are usually in a great deal of pain.

Although the rebounder may be acting with the utmost of sincerity, he or she is really trying to heal from the pain of the previous relationship; and that person may find that healing is difficult or impossible without someone to hold on to. To the rebounder, going it alone is no match for the invigorating feelings that accompany new involvement. If you are, have been, or are likely to be involved with someone who is rebounding, all these emotional factors are important to consider if you're wondering whether your "new" relationship with that person will really last.

However, not everyone who has recently come to the end of a relationship shows the patterns of a rebounder. Those whose relationships were characterized at the end by indifference (emotionally dead for a long time before the actual breakup) could be excellent candidates for immediate involvement. *The true test is whether the person who is rebounding has the ability to regard you as a unique individual—rather than someone who might be a cure for loneliness and isolation.* In that regard, be aware of these other warning signs:

• The rebounder may expect you to make major changes in your life without thoroughly discussing what *your* feelings are. It is important to be aware of anyone who makes demands on you early in a relationship, without being concerned that your needs are being met.

• If the rebounder portrays the estranged spouse or partner in all-negative terms, heed that as a warning sign. It means that he or she is not taking a lot of responsibility for whatever role he or she played in the failure of the relationship. If your potential partner is a chronic blamer, that is an excellent reason to be cautious in and of itself. Or your potential partner's attitude could mean that there is still a high level of emotional involvement with the previous partner, even though it is negative. And it could also mean that once the initial attraction to you begins to wane, you will become the object of some generalized anger meant for that old partner. Moreover, someone who sees himself or herself as carrying no fault or responsibility in the past relationship probably blames others in general for life's woes.

• You are involved with a person who is leaving a relationship through no choice of his/her own. In their passivity, people of this kind are looking more for someone to lean on than to have an adult relationship with. If you are to become that person's crutch, at least make that choice consciously.

Some other examples of rebounders include:

• People who have divorced long ago but still harbor the fantasy of getting back with their ex.
• A person who has been in a long-term relationship and is afraid of being out in "the singles scene." Therefore, it becomes much more desirable for that person to latch on to someone for support.
• Some rebounders leap into the first available relationship as soon as they hear that their ex has become involved or married someone else; that can occur even years after a divorce.

The main danger of involvement with a rebounder is that you will become insignificant once the rebounder begins to feel emotionally stable. To extend the broken leg metaphor: if you have been a crutch, ask yourself what happens to the crutch once the leg heals? Most people who had broken legs tend to throw their crutches away at that point.

In the case of Kenneth and Sandy, their relationship—admittedly a rebound one—ended when she was able to regain her independence. She told Kenneth that she needed time to be her own person and not to be involved so quickly. However, several months later, Kenneth was devastated when Sandy became involved with another man, whom she later married. During the time when she was seeing Kenneth, the leftover issues of her first marriage began to approach resolution. After Sandy had the experience of being independent for a while, she was more capable of entering a relationship that was *not* a rebound one. Kenneth, however, was left with a great deal of pain, because he had not recognized the role he played as Sandy's rebound relationship. As often happens, Kenneth had the illusion that Sandy had already "gotten over" her marriage when she began seeing him. The situation described here is a rather typical one.

PREBOUND RELATIONSHIPS

A prebound relationship is quite similar in dimension to a rebound relationship. However, the prebounder's involvement begins while he or she is still very involved in the last relationship—which is typically an unhappy one, heading toward an end. The prebounder does not want to "go it alone," even for a moment.

The prebound relationship usually begins as a tryst or an affair. Typically, the prebounder "falls in love" and then begins deliberations about what to do with the previous spouse or partner. If you become involved with a prebounder, it is possible that you instinctively want to rescue that person from his or her "unfulfilling home." The rescue impulses may be quite strong. The prebounder will move directly from the previous home right in with you. For a little while the world may become your oyster. However, as the novelty wears off, the true potential for the relationship comes out.

Prebounders are extremely prone to moving back with their ex-partners. Or, since they have had literally no transition between the two relationships, they may simply stay in the nest with you until they feel strong enough to go tackle the world and to try to have that crucial transition time before reinvolvement. Those involved with prebounders are often quite surprised when what they hoped would become a long-term relationship does not make it past a few months. The prebounder who moves on is likely to get involved with someone entirely new sometime down the road. So along with the caution about this kind of relationship goes the suggestion to let little surprise you.

OTHER TYPES OF ONE-SIDED SITUATIONS

So far in this chapter we have considered only those relationships in which there is *inequity* of commitment between partners. In addition to the specific situations I've described, there are some general traits that characterize relationships where the level of commitment differs on each side. Some of these traits may exist to a small degree even in the best of relationships. But use caution when one of these traits seem to characterize a *pattern* between you and your partner. Some signs of inequity:

• You are almost always the one who is giving. Your partner, who is the receiver, just seems insensitive to your needs.

• You are involved with someone who threatens suicide or other dire consequences if you break up with him or her; so you stay involved almost as a form of "emotional ransom."

• You or your partner expect a relationship to fulfill all of your needs; you consider anyone else (even same-sex friends) to be a threat to your involvement. If one-sided restrictions are imposed by one partner, the other is likely to experience the relationship as being too confining.

• You are so afraid of your partner's constant threats to leave if any issue or disagreement comes up, that you devote a good portion of your life to making no waves. At the same time, you realize few of your life goals.

• You are involved with a breeder of low self-esteem who has convinced you of your inadequacy to such a degree that you find *your* self-esteem waning considerably.

• In another version of the above, your partner has such a low sense of self-worth that you practically devote your entire life to building him or her up, to the exclusion of your own goals. You dare not have any accomplishments that will reinforce his or her feelings of inadequacy.

• Your partner is extremely narcissistic—self-involved to the exclusion of you—or requires so much attention that you and your needs literally get lost. You take whatever little tidbits you are able to get from the relationship as though they are morsels of nourishment you cannot do without. The relationship could preempt any goal that you have, yet you stay. As one woman recently put it: "This relationship is similar to that of owning a boat you can't afford. It makes no practical sense, but you won't hear of any alternative that includes doing without it."

• Your partner is extremely immature and abusive, and perhaps does not even *like* you. Yet your partner expects a high level of availability and sexual performance from you. You do not get in return any of what would be expected if the involvement were more mutual.

• You are involved with someone who wants to be a platonic friend, yet you want romantic involvement. One thing that is changing for the better is the acceptance of friendships between men and women in a platonic way. This can work fine unless one of you wants a more intense relationship or a romance. Sometimes the result of this is a pseudosexual relationship: One person would rather just be friends but becomes sexually involved so as not to be rejecting of the friend. If you are in love with someone who considers you merely a friend, chances are that until you are able to direct your romantic feelings elsewhere, the "friendship" will be a very frustrating situation for you.

• You are involved with someone with whom you want a long-term committed relationship, and your partner insists that this is not in the cards; yet you continue to try to change the other person in order to push the relationship where you want it to go.

• Your involvement tends to be with people who, almost by definition, are unavailable. For instance, you are heterosexual, yet you find people who are gay; or, you want children, yet you are in relationships with partners who hate children . . . the list here could be endless. I have even seen instances that include people who are doing life sentences in prison without parole! To the extent that such partners are unwilling or unable to change their situations, such relationships have little chance of succeeding.

If you recognize yourself in any of the descriptions above, ask yourself if you have set things up to the point where it is highly unlikely for you ever to get the fulfillment you want without your having to make some major changes. Taking responsibility for recognizing your patterns is the first step toward changing them.

REASONS YOU MAY BE THRIVING ON ONE-SIDED LOVE AFFAIRS

Why do many people find themselves repeatedly in one-sided love affairs?

Let's say right up front that there are plenty of good people out there to choose from. Let's also say that it is not because you are unlovable, unattractive, or in some other way cursed to remain sans a relationship. I believe that there is someone for everybody. In addition, as I pointed out many times previously, it is possible that your situation can be worked through if your partner is willing to work on the issues with you.

But those who typically enter into or stay in one-sided love affairs do so for many reasons. Some we have already discussed. But there are other reasons, such as:

• *You might tend to be love-prone.* By that I mean you consider yourself a person who habitually falls in love in such a way that you act as though you have no control whatsoever over your emotions. You may even feel as though you catch "love at first sight" almost as though it were some kind of virus. Sometimes it is great to have feelings that are fantasy-based about being involved with someone in a spontaneous way. But the downside is when you are hit with and refuse to accept the reality that whatever it is you are fantasizing about won't go any further. It is only when you insist that *your fantasy must go further* that you get into an entanglement that holds few possibilities. Love-prone people spend a lot of time being hurt, until they accept the reality that having what they fantasized about is not always possible.

• Similar to being love-prone is being a love junkie. In this case, chances are you spend an excessive amount of your life trying somehow to fulfill the needs of others. Those others can certainly include lovers—but also friends, bosses, associates, co-workers, neighbors, and others who are "takers." The object of all this pleasing is to get those people's love and approval. Sometimes a pleaser of this type will settle for any situation in which he or she gets even a crumb of approval.

• You have a *preoccupation with vulnerability in relationships*. Although it has been romanticized that being vulnerable is definitely the way to go, vulnerability also means weakness or the inability to choose. In fact, the word "vulnerability" literally means weak. The best couples are those who can feel deeply for each other while standing on their own two feet. As soon as you give up the ability to stand on your own and to be able to choose, the chances are there will be someone around to exploit you.

• *You are ambivalent about commitment.* On the one hand you want it and seek it; on the other hand you pick the kind of person who gives early signs that commitment is not really for him or her.

• *Your self-esteem is at a level much lower than it needs to be;* as a result, you "melt" in the presence of anyone who gives you the feelings that you believe you need to make you feel whole.

• Perhaps *long-term or committed involvement is not what you want*, but you believe it is what you should want or you "want to want." In any event, your issues bring out the one-sided nature of the relationships you enter. If this is the case, it is possible that by recognizing that fact you can back off a bit and take the time you need in order to ready yourself emotionally.

```
╔══════════════════════════════════╗
║  ADDITIONAL STEPS YOU CAN         ║
║  TAKE TO CHANGE                   ║
║  ONE-SIDED INVOLVEMENT            ║
╚══════════════════════════════════╝
```

This chapter has considered many relationships in which mutuality is difficult or impossible to obtain. No matter how hard you try, there are no sure-fire ways to spark romance where it doesn't exist or to breathe life into a relationship that just isn't working. But for now, let's assume that you want to turn your relationship into one that is more fulfilling. With that in mind, consider these additional points.

• *When it becomes apparent what you want from your partner, ask for it.* Remember, however, that you can only *hope* that he or she will change certain behaviors. *Demanding* that his or her personality change is a dead end.
• *Look at how you hold up your own side of a one-sided or lopsided situation.* Perhaps you need to be giving *less.* Don't be afraid to back off. Sometimes, if mutual feelings aren't present and you cool off, you become a bit more appealing by putting a chill in the air.
• *Set a time limit.* If things don't improve by that time, then recognize the reality that it may be necessary to move on.
• *See if you really have what you want,* rather than focusing on what it is your partner wants or does. Review some of what was said in Chapter 1 about the "Peter Principle."
• *Take a look at who your partner really is versus the fantasy that you harbor about him or her.* Sometimes by talking to someone who knows you both and just looking at the subtleties, you can get that piece of insight that will make your next step more obvious.

• Believe it if someone tells you that they consider you just a friend, that they are not in love with you, that they don't have the feelings for you that you have for them, or that "you are a nice person but . . ." Even though you may not be hearing what you *want* to hear, *stop wasting precious energy trying to change that person's mind.* Remember, every moment you spend in a one-sided love affair is a moment that you don't have available for one that *is* mutual.

• *It is okay to love another person: The problem is when you demand that the other person love you back as well.* If you find yourself obsessed with trying to get mutuality where it does not exist, consider this an issue of your own that deserves top priority. Relationships that work are grounded in reality and mutuality. In fact, reality can represent the potential for you to heal or for you to become more lost in a no-win situation.

You have a choice as to whether to get involved emotionally or otherwise. Your emotions are only one way—although an extremely important part of the way—in which you perceive, evaluate, and judge. Your rational mind is the other. See both points of view, and then step back and make a choice with all things considered. If you can do that, then you will be much less likely to enter or to stay in relationships that are inappropriate—emotionally or otherwise.

CHAPTER EIGHT

CAN YOUR RELATIONSHIP BE SAVED?

If someone were to ask me to make a single statement regarding relationships that comes the closest to absolute certainty, it would have to be this:

> For a relationship to begin or to continue, there has to be a degree of desire and/or effort on the part of both partners; but for a relationship to end, all that is needed is one partner to end it.

This chapter is designed to help you arrive at some perspective as to whether your relationship can be saved—assuming it is at a point where this question needs to be asked. The following is an inventory designed to give you a self-assessment of this most complex question. You may find that this assessment provides you with some additional insight in the way of warning signals, and this insight, in turn, can help you make affirmative choices that could lead to the deepening of the relationship—or to an unambivalent end to it.

Let me suggest that you take this inventory by yourself, using a separate piece of paper. If it is appropriate, have your partner take it as well. When you are completely finished you may want to compare your answers and discuss some of the implications that I address later in the chapter.

> ## CAN YOUR RELATIONSHIP
> ## BE SAVED?—AN INVENTORY

1. My partner and I no longer feel like friends.

   _____YES, this describes my relationship.

   _____NO, this does not describe my relationship.

2. My partner and I have developed a very strong wall that separates us.

   _____YES, this describes my relationship.

   _____NO, this does not describe my relationship.

3. I am constantly thinking about how nice it would be to have an affair.

   _____YES, this describes my relationship.

   _____NO, this does not describe my relationship.

4. When my partner and I fight, it gets nasty and I am left with feelings of wanting to get out.

   _____YES, this describes my relationship.

   _____NO, this does not describe my relationship.

5. My partner has told me at a time other than when we were in the middle of a fight that he/she would be happier if we split up.

   _____YES, this describes my relationship.

   _____NO, this does not describe my relationship.

6. I am unwilling to accept my partner as he/she is. If this relationship is to continue, he/she will have to make some very major changes that he/she is unwilling to make.

    _____YES, this describes my relationship.

    _____NO, this does not describe my relationship.

7. My partner and I have little in common anymore.

    _____YES, this describes my relationship.

    _____NO, this does not describe my relationship.

8. I would leave this relationship in a heartbeat if I felt confident that I could make it on my own or through the painful transition period of a breakup.

    _____YES, this describes my relationship.

    _____NO, this does not describe my relationship.

9. Although I no longer love my partner, I feel responsible for him/her. I think the only thing that is really keeping me there is guilt.

    _____YES, this describes my relationship.

    _____NO, this does not describe my relationship.

10. My partner and I fight a lot, and I fear that underneath the fighting there is not much left.

    _____YES, this describes my relationship.

    _____NO, this does not describe my relationship.

11. When I am about to be around my partner and I think of having to spend time with him/her, I get an empty feeling.

    _____YES, this describes my relationship.

    _____NO, this does not describe my relationship.

12. My partner and I are just no longer playing for the same team.

    _____YES, this describes my relationship.

    _____NO, this does not describe my relationship.

13. The more time goes by, the more I begin to dislike my partner.

    _____YES, this describes my relationship.

    _____NO, this does not describe my relationship.

14. My respect for my partner is practically all gone.

    _____YES, this describes my relationship.

    _____NO, this does not describe my relationship.

15. There is very little trust left in our relationship.

    _____YES, this describes my relationship.

    _____NO, this does not describe my relationship.

16. I constantly fear my partner's abusive behavior. If it happens again, I'm leaving.

    _____YES, this describes my relationship.

    _____NO, this does not describe my relationship.

17. My partner abuses alcohol or drugs. It is even more intolerable to me that he/she denies that the usage is problematic.

    _____YES, this describes my relationship.

    _____NO, this does not describe my relationship.

18. I can only tolerate my partner if one of us is high on alcohol or drugs.

    _____YES, this describes my relationship.

    _____NO, this does not describe my relationship.

19. If I could afford it financially I would leave.

    _____YES, this describes my relationship.

    _____NO, this does not describe my relationship.

20. My partner has an emotional hold on me. I would love to leave but feel too hooked and addicted to the relationship.

_____YES, this describes my relationship.

_____NO, this does not describe my relationship.

21. My partner has children whom he/she expects me to relate to. The relationship would be fine if they were not there, but they are here to stay and it is creating a very unhappy situation for me.

_____YES, this describes my relationship.

_____NO, this does not describe my relationship.

22. I should want my relationship to continue, or I want to want my relationship to continue, but I can't say that I do want it to continue.

_____YES, this describes my relationship.

_____NO, this does not describe my relationship.

23. We are unable to resolve our differences, but my partner refuses to enter counseling or therapy.

_____YES, this describes my relationship.

_____NO, this does not describe my relationship.

24. My partner has told me that he/she doesn't love me anymore.

_____YES, this describes my relationship.

_____NO, this does not describe my relationship.

25. My partner has done something for which I cannot forgive him/her. That was the straw that broke the camel's back.

_____YES, this describes my relationship.

_____NO, this does not describe my relationship.

26. We just have so many differences that it is overwhelming to think we can even begin to address them.

_____YES, this describes my relationship.

_____NO, this does not describe my relationship.

27. I am so overwhelmed by my partner and his/her constant demands for love and approval, perfectionism, and/or rigid rules of just how the relationship should be and how each of us should behave within it, that I sometimes want to give up.

    _____YES, this describes my relationship.

    _____NO, this does not describe my relationship.

28. I am almost certain my partner is having an affair and if he/she is, I will not tolerate it.

    _____YES, this describes my relationship.

    _____NO, this does not describe my relationship.

29. I feel closer to my partner when we are not together.

    _____YES, this describes my relationship.

    _____NO, this does not describe my relationship.

30. There is definitely more pain than joy or pleasure associated with my partner and our relationship.

    _____YES, this describes my relationship.

    _____NO, this does not describe my relationship.

31. This relationship has become a constant burden.

    _____YES, this describes my relationship.

    _____NO, this does not describe my relationship.

32. If I knew I could find another mate, I would leave immediately.

    _____YES, this describes my relationship.

    _____NO, this does not describe my relationship.

33. I am having an affair with someone I value much more than my partner. I am unwilling to give this other person up under any circumstances.

    _____YES, this describes my relationship.

    _____NO, this does not describe my relationship.

34. I feel very indifferent toward my partner and have little motivation to try and work things out.

    _____YES, this describes my relationship.

    _____NO, this does not describe my relationship.

35. My most stress-free moments are when my partner and I are separated.

    _____YES, this describes my relationship.

    _____NO, this does not describe my relationship.

36. My partner and I are totally inflexible with each other.

    _____YES, this describes my relationship.

    _____NO, this does not describe my relationship.

37. I don't even have a desire to tell my partner how I feel anymore—positive or negative.

    _____YES, this describes my relationship.

    _____NO, this does not describe my relationship.

38. Our relationship has peaked and could never again be as good as it was.

    _____YES, this describes my relationship.

    _____NO, this does not describe my relationship.

39. When I think of us growing old together, life seems not worth living.

    _____YES, this describes my relationship.

    _____NO, this does not describe my relationship.

40. At this point, there is just too much water under the bridge.

    _____YES, this describes my relationship.

    _____NO, this does not describe my relationship.

EVALUATION

If you thought that I was going to ask you to count the number of questions in which you answered yes and then give you a range where your marriage is safe, where it is potentially in trouble, or where it's doomed, don't be disappointed, but it is not quite that simple. *Any* of the above questions to which you answered yes could mean your relationship is either already destroyed or heading for destruction.

What needs to be looked at are the issues that came to your mind when you answered that *yes* describes your situation. This is especially true of "yes" items that come up constantly or with great intensity in your relationship. You may be noticing "warning signs" in items that apply to your situation to a milder degree. In that case, the item in question could be a developing threat, but you have caught it in time.

Below are the questions along with the degree of risk a "yes" answer usually represents, and some direction to the part of this book that explores the issue represented.

1. My partner and I no longer feel like friends.

   Moderate risk: see Chapter 4, Chapter 6, and Chapter 14.

2. My partner and I have developed a very strong wall that separates us.

   High risk: See Chapter 5, Chapter 6, and Chapter 12.

3. I am constantly thinking about how nice it would be to have an affair.

   Moderate risk: See Chapter 7 and Chapter 10.

4. When my partner and I fight, it gets nasty and I am left with feelings of wanting to get out.

   Moderate risk: See Chapter 5.

5. My partner told me at a time other than when we were in the middle of a fight that he/she would be happier if we split up.

   High risk: See Chapter 5 and Chapter 13.

6. I am unwilling to accept my partner as he/she is. If this relationship is to continue, he/she will have to make some very major changes that he/she is unwilling to make.

   High risk: See Chapter 1, Chapter 12, and Chapter 13.

7. My partner and I have little in common anymore.

   Moderate risk: See Chapter 1 and Chapter 6.

8. I would leave this relationship in a heartbeat if I felt confident that I could make it on my own or through the painful transition period of a breakup.

   High risk: See Chapter 13.

9. Although I no longer love my partner, I feel responsible for him/her. I think the only thing that is really keeping me there is guilt.

   High risk: See Chapter 12 and Chapter 13.

10. My partner and I fight a lot, and I fear that underneath the fighting there is not much left.

    Moderate risk: See Chapter 5 and Chapter 6.

11. When I am about to be around my partner and I think of having to spend time with him/her, I get an empty feeling in my stomach.

    High risk: See Chapter 6, Chapter 8, and Chapter 12.

12. My partner and I are just no longer playing for the same team.

    Moderate risk: See Chapter 4, Chapter 6, and Chapter 12.

13. The more time goes by, the more I begin to dislike my partner.

    High risk: See Chapter 1, Chapter 6, and Chapter 13.

14. My respect for my partner is practically all gone.

    High risk: See Chapter 5 and Chapter 6.

15. There is very little trust left in our relationship.

    High risk: See Chapter 5, Chapter 9, and Chapter 10.

16. I constantly fear my partner's abusive behavior. If it happens again, I'm leaving.

    High risk: See Chapter 5 and Chapter 13.

17. My partner abuses alcohol or drugs. It is even more intolerable to me that he/she denies that the usage is problematic.

    High risk: See Chapter 5 and Chapter 6.

18. I can only tolerate my partner if one of us is high on alcohol or drugs.

    High risk: See Chapter 5.

19. If I could afford it financially I would leave.

    Moderate risk: See Chapter 5, Chapter 12, and Chapter 13.

20. My partner has an emotional hold on me. I would love to leave but feel too hooked and addicted to the relationship.

    High risk: See Chapter 5 and Chapter 13.

21. My partner has children whom he/she expects me to relate to. The relationship would be fine if they were not there, but they are here to stay and it is creating a very unhappy situation for me.

    Moderate risk: See Chapter 4 and Chapter 12.

22. I should want my relationship to continue, or I want to want my relationship to continue, but I can't say that I do want it to continue.

    High risk: See Chapter 1, Chapter 7, and Chapter 13.

23. We are unable to resolve our differences, but my partner refuses to enter counseling or therapy.

    Moderate risk: See Chapter 4, Chapter 5, and Chapter 8.

24. My partner has told me that he/she doesn't love me anymore.

    Moderate risk: See Chapter 6 and Chapter 12.

25. My partner has done something for which I cannot forgive him/her. That was the straw that broke the camel's back.

    High risk: See Chapter 5 and Chapter 10.

26. We just have so many differences that it is overwhelming to think that we can even begin to address them.

    Moderate risk: See Chapter 3, Chapter 4, Chapter 5, Chapter 6, Chapter 10, and Chapter 11.

27. I am so overwhelmed by my partner and his/her constant demands for love and approval, perfectionism, and/or rigid rules of just how the relationship should be and how each of us should behave in it, that I sometimes want to give up.

    Moderate risk: See Chapter 1, Chapter 7, and Chapter 9.

28. I am almost certain my partner is having an affair and if he/she is, I will not tolerate it.

    Moderate risk: See Chapter 9 and Chapter 10.

29. I feel closer to my partner when we are not together.

    Moderate risk: See Chapter 6 and Chapter 14.

30. There is definitely more pain than joy or pleasure associated with my partner and our relationship.

    Moderate risk: See Chapter 5.

31. This relationship has become a constant burden.

    High risk: See Chapter 4, Chapter 5, and Chapter 13.

32. If I knew I could find another mate, I would leave immediately.

    High risk: See Chapter 5, Chapter 6, Chapter 7, Chapter 10, Chapter 12, and Chapter 13.

33. I am having an affair with someone I value much more than my partner. I am unwilling to give this other person up under any circumstances.

    High risk: See Chapter 7, Chapter 10, and Chapter 13.

34. I am very indifferent toward my partner and have little motivation to try and work things out.

    High risk: See Chapter 6 and Chapter 13.

35. My most stress-free moments are when my partner and I are separated.

    Moderate risk: See Chapter 8, Chapter 13, and Chapter 14.

36. My partner and I are totally inflexible with each other.

    Moderate risk: See Chapter 1, Chapter 2, and Chapter 5.

37. I don't even have a desire to tell my partner how I feel anymore—positive or negative.

    High risk: See Chapter 6, Chapter 8, and Chapter 13.

38. Our relationship has peaked and could never again be as good as it was.

    Low risk: See Chapter 1, Chapter 3, and Chapter 14.

39. When I think of us growing old together, life seems not worth living.

High risk: See Chapter 6, Chapter 13, and Chapter 14.

40. At this point, there is just too much water under the bridge.

Moderate risk: See Chapter 4, Chapter 5, and Chapter 10.

MAKING THE DETERMINATION

At the time that I went through my own separation and divorce in the early seventies, I took issue with the idea that my marriage had been a failure. Indeed it yielded a wonderful child. It was certainly a source of pleasure for a significant period of time; the dividend was a great deal of learning and personal growth. I certainly didn't feel like a failure. I refused to write off the entire four-and-a-half years as a marriage that never should have happened. True, my marriage *failed to continue*—but so do many meaningful experiences in life.

After a lot of thought, I came up with what I consider a much better explanation. It helped me to put the experience into perspective—and I have seen it do the same for countless numbers of people I have seen in my practice, spoken with on the radio, and met at my talks and seminars. It is the idea that *relationships that end do so, not out of failure, but merely because they have run their course.*

Perhaps you have seen other important elements of your life run their course: a job, a career, or a lifestyle that you once cherished yet that didn't seem to fit as you got older and your life changed. Or think about your family of origin. If you have now left that home, does it mean that your family relationship "failed"? Of course not: That time of your life simply ran its course. Though that transition was possibly a difficult one, it doesn't mean you regret it.

If after taking the self-assessment inventory you have determined that your relationship has run its course, you may want to go right to Chapter 13, which is devoted entirely to the steps you can take that will help you to make what you have decided is a necessary transition.

However, even if you are still hopeful about saving your relationship, consider these additional points.

• If both of you are willing to work on (by whatever means) the most serious issues, *your relationship is still viable.* In the self-evaluation you had the opportunity to define these issues and consider whether they spelled high or moderate risk. Can you pinpoint the issues that got you this far? If you and your partner can at least agree what the categories of your issues and problems are, you'll be taking a significant step toward working together on your relationship. Theoretically, what would have to happen for your relationship to get better?

• If your partner is unwilling to make certain changes that you have talked about, does the same apply to you as well? Are there things that both you and your partner can do together to give more life to your relationship? Are either of you being inflexible at this point? If your partner is the only one who is being inflexible, what are you willing to do that can demonstrate flexibility? If changes by neither one of you are on the horizon, can you learn to accept things the way they are? If this is the only major sacrifice you have to make, are you willing to do it for the sake of saving the relationship?

• What does your relationship mean to you at this point? What exactly is it that you need from your partner? What is it you are willing to give in return? If your relationship never gets better, what would be your next step? What are your minimum criteria for determining that your relationship is salvageable? What are your partner's?

• Who do you want your partner to be that he or she is not? Your best friend? Someone toward whom you can feel more sexual? Share more intimacies? Someone with whom you can merely lead a peaceful coexistence?

• Are you holding an unworkable relationship together merely out of the fear of being alone? For the kids? (See Chapter 12, which is entirely devoted to this issue.) For financial reasons? Out of a guilt for what will happen to your partner if you make the unilateral decision to leave?

The questions above have no "right" or pat answers. They are designed for you and your partner to discuss together—as well as for each of you to think about separately.

The following points may help to stimulate the process for you, as they have for many others.

• Many people think that in order to end a relationship, you literally have to despise the individual from whom you are separating—or, at the very least, not consider their feelings to be important. Not so. With rare exceptions, a relationship that is not serving both of you is not benefiting either of you in the long run. While you may still care deeply for your partner, at the same time you may become aware that the relationship is just not workable.

• One rarely, if ever, makes a significant change merely because his or her partner demands that those changes be made. Promises are often made to appease the other—and so are temporary changes. Permanent changes are made for oneself, not another. Unless you and your partner truly desire to make the changes that need to be made in order to save your relationship, at the very best you will only prolong it. Changes will be permanent only if your partner clearly sees where it is to his or her personal advantage to make them.

• If your decision is to end the relationship . . . remember, there may be many times when you will second-guess your decision. There may even be times, later on, when you will regret it. And, yet, waiting for certainty can take up a significant portion of your life. Even in the most difficult situations, it is often easier in the short run to stay in an unworkable situation than to face the immediate pain of separation.

• However, if either of you simply no longer wants this relationship, it is highly unlikely that it can continue as anything other than a perfunctory living arrangement. When do you *know* that a relationship has run its course? Three signals should be taken very seriously:

1. You and/or your partner do not want to stay in the relationship, and you have no desire to work on resolving the issues.
2. There is no longer a desire for both of you to spend time together—and neither of you feels motivated to increase your tolerance of each other, work on your indifference, or be involved in each other's lives.
3. The magnitude of stress is so great that it causes you physical or emotional problems that can be attributed to the relationship. (Often the distress disappears when you are not together.)

Of course, as I pointed out earlier, you can stay together for a lifetime as long as you don't require the relationship to be more than what it is. Indeed, many do make a lifelong commitment based on religion, financial necessity, convenience, or just because of their unwillingness to make the change, or fear of going it alone for a while. While this is not the choice preferred by most, as we will explore in Chapter 12, it has certainly become the choice of many.

IF YOU ARE STILL UNDECIDED

Many times in my practice I have seen people who stayed in relationships for inordinate periods of time, even though they would later say their relationships were totally unworkable. While the main purpose of this book is to help you to stay together, this goal is important only to the extent that your relationship adds some amount of happiness to your life. Each day we spend in an unhappy relationship is one day less we will have to spend in one that brings us a realistic amount of passion, comfort, and happiness.

If you are still in limbo about whether your relationship can work or not in the long term, consider the following alternatives.

• *Set a time limit.* Most relationships that aren't working are characterized by a great deal of fighting, distance, or indifference. Nobody is happy, and yet there is no immediate pressure to break up or to take steps to turn things around. By determining that if things don't get better within a specified period of time you will separate, many couples find that their relationship becomes a higher priority. Practice has shown that this simple agreement is most effective when the couple actually set a date. Once you have a specific amount of time, each person can make his or her best effort to save the relationship, knowing there is the reality of a possible breakup.

On the other hand, there is sometimes a sense of relief once this agreement is made and an end is on the horizon; that, too, tells you a great deal about where your relationship really is.

• *Trial separations.* An intermission can be helpful when at least one partner determines that it would be best not to have the other around for a while. Will the absence draw them together or push them further apart? At best, a trial separation has a built-in time limit (a week, a month, six months), which enables each party to think through (as well as act out) his or her options without the finality of the relationship being over. In addition, it gives both a vacation from whatever chronic issues are making the potential separation imminent. During a separation, people often get a clearer picture of who their partners really are.

By taking the edge off of the tension you feel together and by giving yourselves a bit of breathing room, choices become clearer. Would you still prefer to go your separate ways once the practical issues have been resolved? Or is coming back together a valid option? Trial separations can be extended indefinitely until one or both of you have a clear perspective of what you want for the long term. I have seen trial separations last as short a period of time as a few hours (going either way) and, at the other extreme, one case in which a "trial" separation lasted twenty years.

• *Get professional help.* Often couples' therapy begins with the question of whether the relationship can or should be saved. Therefore, all three entities are considered: each partner (that's two), and the couple as a separate entity is the third. A therapist is an impartial observer who often can help you to access the strengths and weaknesses of the relationship and of each partner, as well as each partner's potential to provide fulfillment to the other. So therapy can be either a vehicle for airing the issues in safety, healing the relationship, or for helping either or both partners to handle whatever issues they face in breaking up, if it is determined that you cannot work out your differences.

If you have opted to enter therapy or counseling and your partner has been unwilling, it might be a good idea for you to make an appointment on your own to discuss the situation. Often a therapist can help you to develop a strategy to bring your partner into the process. If you yourself have been in individual therapy and your partner objects to going to see your therapist, honor that objection and find a person who will be acceptable to both of you. Your own therapist may be as impartial as can be, even if you have been in individual therapy with that person for quite a while. However, your partner may not believe that this is the case and may fear being ganged up on. This is especially true if you are a lot more therapy-wise than is your partner. When this is the case, the best course of action may be to let your partner pick the therapist.

Most importantly, it is unwise to let any stone go unturned when it comes to saving a relationship that you value. Millions have been helped by couples therapy, both when the relationship could be saved and when help is needed with the transition of getting out. Moreover, it is rare when it does harm. I cannot urge you strongly enough to give this a try at any point in your relationship when problems you cannot seem to resolve surface. But certainly at the point where you see a breakup as the only way to resolve your present difficulties.

Being in limbo is a state of mind, not a point of fact. Getting out of limbo may not be easy, but once you do you have the rest of your life to gain.

If the inventory at the beginning of this chapter was helpful, I would urge you to try it more than once. You might want to read it again six months from now—or a year from now—and ask yourself: "Does our relationship look more hopeful? Have we really talked about the issues that are most critical? Do we feel closer to each other now than we did before?"

If so, it's a positive sign for your relationship. And, remember, to the extent that you understand what your issues are and work with each other, your relationship has the potential to grow steadily stronger.

PART THREE

Choices and Issues

CHAPTER NINE

JEALOUSY:

Insecurity or Caring?

Jealousy has not been called the green-eyed monster for nothing.

Norma and John had a marriage that worked remarkably well for both of them, but they had one ever present issue that they had been unable to resolve: jealousy. It was Norma's first marriage, John's second; and they had been together for a little over four years when their marriage hit a crisis. One thing they both agreed about was the cause of the crisis—jealousy.

"I get absolutely furious when I think John is flirting with another woman—or if someone comes on to him," Norma said. "I try to pretend that it doesn't bother me, but it does, and when John makes light of the situation, that bothers me even more."

John's response was more complex. He appeared pleased at the idea of Norma being so "emotionally vested" in their relationship that she would feel threatened. He considered his flirtations harmless. But he didn't like the "side of Norma" that emerged when she was jealous.

"This jealousy brings out a side of you that is really ugly!" he said to her at an early session. "Sometimes it is like you are going to get up and *leave*, right on the spot. I can't understand what's so threatening to you." John added, "If we could only get a handle on this, we wouldn't need to fight about it. There's just no *reason* to be jealous."

For John and Norma, the "handle" involved each of them understanding the other's view of jealousy. When Norma saw John flirting, his behavior triggered an almost primal sense of insecurity. John, on the other hand, could never understand "what the big deal is."

In part, their different views evolved from differing experience with relationships. John and Norma first met while John was still married to his first wife. John described the final years of his first marriage—before he met Norma—as being alternately stormy and indifferent. He and his first wife would sometimes discuss splitting up, but then, for lack of motivation, they would abandon the idea. Although his prior marriage was in John's words "destined to end," he didn't really consider divorce a possibility until he met Norma. When he did, divorce soon became an inevitability.

John met Norma at work, and their relationship began with mild flirtations. They found each other extremely attractive. After several months, they each were fantasizing a love affair, and not long after that they shared their fantasies with each other. John found himself experiencing feelings he had never previously had for a woman. He knew then it would just be a matter of time before he left his wife, and married Norma.

For Norma, her romance and subsequent marriage to John presented no dilemma whatsoever. She has said repeatedly that she knew, almost from the first time they met, that John was "the one."

Norma attributed her jealous rages to the deep and intense feelings she felt for John. But a closer examination revealed that there were some unresolved trust issues connected with the fact that he had left his first wife for her. From Norma's point of view, John had already proved that he wasn't above seeing another woman and leaving his wife for someone else. "If he did it to her, who's to say he won't do it to me?" Norma asked.

That revelation helped Norma to put her feelings into perspective. John tried to explain why his first marriage happened in the first place, and why it had not been "destined to work."

"We were two confused kids," he said. "We wanted to get out of our parents' homes." (He was twenty-one at the time, his wife was eighteen.) "I never knew what I should even look for in a relationship until I met Norma," he said.

From John's point of view, he had never given Norma any reason to doubt his fidelity or his commitment to their relationship.

Once Norma and John both made the connection between her past suspicions and her present insecurity, the couple had the perspective they needed. John could begin to see how Norma viewed his innocent flirtations as something far more significant—a real threat to her security in the marriage.

It is a rare relationship that has not at one time or another hosted some degree of jealousy: Your partner looks affectionately at a much younger, more shapely, taller, more muscular (you fill in the blanks), member of the opposite sex. What are some situations that can initiate feelings of jealousy?

• The two of you are at a party together. Your partner spends an inordinate amount of time talking to a member of the opposite sex to whom you are not introduced.
• Your partner gets a sexy (perhaps even inappropriate) gift from someone at the office for Christmas.
• Your partner talks glowingly about a past relationship in a way that you find upsetting.
• Your partner finally stops asking you to take up golf and enters a foursome where two of the other players are attractive members of the opposite sex.
• Your partner has lunch with an old flame. That night he or she would rather go to sleep than make love with you.

Usually, jealousy is initiated when you feel threatened by the possibility that your partner is *not* exclusively committed to you—either psychologically, emotionally, or sexually. Although you might be jealous of a current friendship or flirtation, you can become just as jealous at the prospect of your deepest fears being realized sometime in the unforeseen future. Or perhaps you are even as jealous of some person who may not even exist as you would be of a real live person your partner has admitted feeling attracted to on some level. To some extent, there is usually at least a subtle sense of mistrust when you feel jealous. Some profound psychological contortions may result from this mistrust. Every emotion possible can be triggered—anger, rage, depression, fear, anxiety, or longing. These negative feelings might be directed toward your partner or toward the person you think your partner is attracted to—whether or not that person even exists!

Jealousy can also be a signal that you are taking each other for granted. For some people, feelings of jealousy put them in touch with the reality that all relationships are mortal entities. After all, in reality, each of us is on some level in competition with every other member of our sex whom our partner sees or meets. If you think about it, this even includes media personages.

WHY ARE WE JEALOUS?

Since jealousy means different things to different people, it follows that it's an emotion that can have many different routes. The degree to which you can handle your jealousy will probably depend on how thoroughly you understand why you feel it in the first place. What are some possible reasons?

• You believe that jealous feelings and romantic feelings are inseparable and that a person who does not have some jealousy in connection with his or her relationship does not deeply care for the other person.

• You suspect your partner precisely because you feel guilty about your own potential for "infidelity." In other words, you are attracted to others outside the relationship; and the lack of trust you feel about yourself then becomes projected onto your partner.

• You believe that you do not compare favorably to anyone your partner finds the least bit attractive. In this case, it could be your self-esteem that is the culprit.

• You suspect that something is in fact wrong in your relationship; and therefore it seems quite possible that the relationship is being hurt by your partner's lack of fidelity. This is true especially if you have not been jealous in the past, but you find yourself becoming increasingly suspicious of and threatened by your partner's outside contacts.

• You fear losing your partner to such a degree that the thought of being without him or her becomes an obsession.

• You believe that each person has just a certain amount of love and that any love, or even interest for that matter, that is shown or thought to be directed by your partner toward another person will leave you longing for the missing affection.

• You have never had the experience of being able to flirt harmlessly with a member of the opposite sex; you believe that no one, especially your partner, is able to enjoy harmless flirtation.

• You believe, as Norma did, that your partner is predisposed to infidelity on the basis of how his or her last relationship ended. This could be the case especially if his or her prior partner lost out to *you*—as was the case with John and Norma.

• You think of your partner in extremely possessive terms and simply don't want to share him or her on any level.

• You become jealous of your partner merely because he or she expresses feelings of jealousy toward you: This becomes a game that the two of you play.

• Perhaps you were a witness to infidelity in your parents' marriage. It could be that you have read, heard about, or witnessed so many situations where trust led to heartbreak, that you have simply resolved (consciously or unconsciously) that you can never let down your guard. If you do (you may believe), you're just asking for immense pain when the "inevitable" occurs. The belief is that no one or that members of your own sex cannot ultimately be exclusive in any relationship.

If you can identify with some of these characteristics of jealousy, perhaps you can begin to separate your beliefs about your partner's actions from the reality of what he or she is actually doing. A major step toward resolving your jealousy is to determine which of these attitudes you are unwilling to give up and which you would like to change. If you can discuss those attitudes with your partner, you may be surprised at how relieved you can both feel when you identify some of the insecurities that lie beneath the surface. Can you agree to work together toward giving up certain attitudes and beliefs? If so, you may be able to make great strides in beginning to resolve some jealousy issues.

INSECURITY? CARING? OR BOTH?

In working with many couples, I have seen jealousy wreak far more havoc on significantly more relationships than provide anything that resembles a source of pleasure. After all, jealousy is grounded on a near impossibility—that is, the demand that your partner give you *psychological exclusivity*.

I doubt that anyone can do that. Ironically, I have rarely met someone who was troubled by their own inability to grant complete mental exclusivity to their partner. Yet many expect their partners to demonstrate that kind of exclusivity toward them.

Is it possible that you became jealous when you are insecure about your relationship? Perhaps jealousy *is* insecurity. The following are some significant indications that this is the case.

• Jealousy is accompanied by negative feelings such as anger, rage, anxiety, and mistrust.

• It is accompanied by the attitude that says, "I am entitled to 100 percent exclusivity on all levels. This can also be accompanied by extreme feelings of possessiveness.

• Jealousy can assume pathological proportions. You believe that your partner is cheating on you, although there is absolutely no concrete or implied evidence. At its most extreme, suspicion and jealousy of this kind have been known to provoke violence toward a partner, a suspected third party, or both.

• You are angered by your partner's *lack* of jealousy. For example, if you put your partner down because he or she refuses to act jealous no matter what you do, you may be interpreting this lack of jealousy to mean lack of commitment.

• You find that jealousy is zapping the fun out of nearly every aspect of your relationship. In other words, you are continually thinking of people to be jealous of, or you are imagining possible scenarios in which your partner can become unfaithful.

Jealousy that has these characteristics can be taken to extremes, and there's unlikely to be a great deal of comfort if one or both partners feel this insecure all the time. The partner who is this jealous is likely to be suspicious and overly demanding, while the partner subjected to extreme jealousy is likely to feel oppressed or angered by the other's demands and watchfulness.

On the other hand, there are other forms of jealousy that may arise as a matter of course in the relationship. Though not necessarily beneficial, this brand of jealousy can be seen as a sign of caring rather than of possessiveness or insecurity.

The case for jealousy as caring can be made if:

• Your jealousy is part of the romantic climate between you and your partner that you enjoy. Some couples get pleasure out of fantasizing together that someone is trying to get between them, and fails.

• As I pointed out earlier, some small degree of jealousy is normal in practically every relationship. It is possible that you believe that a couple who is somehow immune to all jealousy does not have a strong relationship. There is nothing wrong with these spoken or unspoken rules as long as they are not more a source of pain than pleasure for you.

• Some couples find that twinges of jealous feelings add to their feelings of passion toward their partner. This is true even when those feelings are not shared with your partner.

However, jealous feelings that are repeatedly expressed to your partner can become *self-fulfilling prophecies.* As the wife of a very jealous husband recently told me: "I had been accused of running around for so long, that when the opportunity presented itself I more or less shrugged my shoulders and said 'okay.' I just had to see what I was missing. Since I was being accused of having affairs anyway, I thought—why not?" While it would be erroneous for her to shirk the responsibility for her own behavior, no one can deny that this woman felt her husband's constant accusations were totally unfair. "I was angry," she added. "I was accused and tried before I even did anything. I'm sure I wanted to prove I could do anything I wanted to. Since he's going to be jealous anyway, what does it matter?"

Just as there is no guarantee that your relationship will stay together, there is no guarantee that your partner will never fall for someone else. If this is going to happen, jealousy can often provide the push that a chain of events needs in order to become reality.

If you are involved in a relationship where the jealousy is constant, and you are always threatened by the possibility that your partner may become involved with someone else, that may be an indication that your jealousy is a healthy symptom of something very wrong in your relationship. To the extent that you have a committed relationship with an agreement of monogamy, there is certainly reason to expect the same degree of fidelity from your partner. If you have agreed upon monogamy, yet you feel that your partner is less committed than you are, it may be important to look at other aspects of your relationship. Watching suspiciously or constantly doubting your partner will not heal the relationship. In fact, it may have just the opposite effect of making your partner feel trapped or unappreciated.

In the final analysis, only you can assess whether your jealousy is an insecurity that is in your best interest to work through and shed, a sign of caring for your partner, or a symptom that something is really going wrong in the relationship.

My own feeling about jealousy is that to the extent that it causes pain, it is generally an insecurity you would be much better off without. To the extent that you can use it as a fantasy device to enrich your lives—enjoy! If you experience jealousy both ways, then you are doubtlessly aware of the complexity of this emotion.

OTHER POSSIBLE OBJECTS OF JEALOUSY

When Angela became involved with Richard, she particularly liked the fact that he did not spend excessive amounts of time with his male friends. What she was not prepared for, however, was the fact that he had several female friends he enjoyed spending time with. Some of the female friends were former lovers; with others he had always maintained purely platonic relationships. Although she'd never suspected Richard of being unfaithful—and, actually, never had a reason to—her feelings of jealousy got the upper hand when he told her about his female friends.

Eventually, Angela was able to change her attitude toward Richard and his female friends. She realized that for the sake of the relationship, she would need to find ways to accept those friendships. However, she was able to *accept* the situation long before she was *comfortable* with it. Only as the relationship stood the test of time was she able to finally become comfortable with it.

Angela had never had a male friend with whom she did not have some degree of romantic attachment. In addition, most of her female friends believed that men and women could not be friends without eventually becoming romantically involved. As her trust of Richard deepened, Angela opened up to a new way of thinking about members of the opposite sex.

The best relationships are not one-stop shops. In my experience, the happiest couples are those who know what it is that they can give to and get from each other. Ideally, they can give each other the freedom to go outside the relationship to share certain activities with others who have the same interests.

But I have seen many couples in which one partner is jealous of most outside relationships—not just those of a romantic nature. The following relationships may arouse jealousy:

* Friends of either sex. You may resent your partner spending time with friends rather than with you alone. Or you resent your partner sharing things about your lives that you believe should remain between the two of you.

* Family members with whom your partner is more involved than you are. The objects of your jealousy can include your own newborn children or children from a previous marriage. Or you may be jealous that your spouse spends time with parents or siblings that you think should be spent with you.

* Co-workers with whom your partner works closely. Opposite sex co-workers are often a great source of jealousy. Obviously, there's always the potential for affairs to develop out of professional relationships. Such romances are very well documented. Moreover, in many situations, co-workers share special bonds. You may find that this kind of closeness is difficult to understand, and you might feel hurt that your partner obviously enjoys these bonds from which you may be excluded.

Any association that your partner undertakes that you are not a part of has the potential for triggering those jealous feelings. The idea that your partner is allocating time elsewhere can lead to the thought that he or she is putting someone else first. The next step in that progression is believing that your partner cares more for someone outside your relationship than for you. It certainly is not hard to see how this can get out of hand. Working out this issue often requires compromise.

Good relationships are not defined by time, possessiveness, or total exclusivity in all spheres. Instead, they are defined by the degree to which each partner can care about the things that are important to the other. If you can talk about your views of what's most important to you—and hear your partner's views—you may develop a very rich understanding of what other relationships mean to each of you. These perspectives may render jealousy unnecessary.

THE PARTNER WHO FLIRTS

Whether we are talking about your partner flirting or your flirtatious behavior, which angers your partner, no chapter on jealousy would be complete without considering some of the implications of flirting.

Flirting is quite normal. So much so, that we often do it unconsciously. In fact, people who flirt often don't realize they are flirting unless someone else (such as their partner) brings it to their attention. The partner who flirts in your presence is probably not acting in any way that's meant to be malicious. Some couples have actually learned to incorporate sexual fantasies of flirtatious behavior into their sex lives.

In my experience, couples who are very secure can even share with each other the idea that they have crushes on people outside the relationship. This is a great way to take something that is potentially threatening and reduce it to the harmless reality that it probably is. If you are bothered by your partner's flirting (assuming it is not done to an extreme degree), it could be that you are not actually threatened by the fact that your partner has thoughts of being unfaithful. Your discomfort could be based on the fact that you find your partner's flirting to be an embarrassment.

This problem can be worked out so that everyone wins. Instead of condemning your partner, what if you simply ask him or her not to be so open about flirting. Share the feelings you have about your partner's flirtatious behavior in a way that will make your partner want to be positively responsive to you rather than defensive. If he or she considers your reaction to be a groundless accusation, there's the danger that your partner may turn the harmless flirting into an all-out competition to see whether he or she can get you upset. What an exercise in mutual unfulfillment—not to mention a source of negative energy. Competition of that kind can eventually have devastating consequences for both of you! Instead, you might focus on the pleasures of flirting in ways that your partner can share. Remember, if your partner finds someone else attractive—but clearly finds *you* even more so—isn't that in reality a compliment? And there are ways for you to get that message across to your partner as well!

TOWARD OVERCOMING JEALOUSY

If indeed you recognize jealousy as an insecurity, there are ways to address this issue with your partner, even though it is very much a personal issue. But when you do talk about your insecurity, you are likely to need many of the communications skills and methods of handling disagreements that I discussed earlier in the book. Because insecurity can become such an all-encompassing feeling, it's essential to keep the following realities in mind when talking to your partner:

• Mental exclusivity is rare. It is quite possible that *you* find other people attractive in ways that would threaten your partner, if he or she knew. So it's only reasonable that your partner may have similar thoughts directed at someone other than you. Give your partner, as well as yourself, equal permission to be human.

• If your partner is really going to act on his or her fantasies and go outside of the relationship, whether it is simply to have a tryst or to become involved in a full-blown affair, in reality there is little you can do about it. You might pretend that you can "do something" by worrying and obsessing, but that doesn't change the situation. Remember that potential for a self-fulfilling prophecy. If you have opposite-sex friends and confidants, be aware of the tendency that I have often seen for one partner to "punish" the other by pretending that something just might be going on when actually there isn't. This manner of hurting your partner can also have very negative consequences.

• If your partner is jealous of others with whom you spend time, make a special effort to show your partner that you are not putting anyone else first. Your partner may reasonably feel excluded if your activities with others are a mystery. If you can show your partner how it is to his or her advantage for you to enjoy certain activities with other people, you will go a long way toward building your comfort level together.

• Comparing the relationship you or your partner may have had with old flames to the one you have now will rarely shed any light, but will almost always produce heat.

• Do you find yourself harboring a lot of negative feelings over someone who is attracted to your partner? Remember, that attraction is meaningless unless your partner reciprocates. Avoid the trap of being threatened by someone merely because he or she has the same taste in people you do.

• If you are constantly intimidated by the prospect of being compared to others, chances are your own self-esteem needs a boost. The fact is, you don't need to be any better than you are to "hold on" to your partner. You can only be who you are—nothing more or less. While this may seem self-evident, many people who feel intimidated try to make themselves over in order to compete for the loyalty of a partner.

• If all else fails, look at the real level of trust you have with your partner and at the reality of the situation. Is there really a threat? If trust is missing in your relationship, that lack of trust could be the thing that does you in. *Don't let it go that far.* And, if it does, make restoring that trust your number-one priority.

Jealousy is the type of negative emotion that you can best work through if you attack it where it is—within you. After all, if there was anything else you could do about it, can't we say that you probably would have done it by now?

But, you may be asking, what happens when your feelings of jealousy are well grounded?

That is the issue I will address in Chapter 10.

CHAPTER TEN

MONOGAMY/ SYNOGAMY:

Variations and Alternatives

Monogamy refers to the practice (or agreement) of exclusivity or fidelity that exists between two partners. Our culture overwhelmingly endorses monogamy as the preferred lifestyle of couples who are married or in other types of committed love relationships. There always have been, and probably will be, cultures, subcultures, and countercultures in which some group (usually the more elite) practices something other than monogamy. Nonetheless, monogamy is generally regarded as the norm in our culture.

There are several variations of monogamy, which include:

• *Traditional monogamy.* An all-encompassing term that refers to a relationship that is grounded in the sanctity and commitment of the traditional marriage.

• *Sexual monogamy.* The agreement or understanding that you will be sexually exclusive with your partner.

• *Emotional monogamy.* The recognition that there is a level of intimacy that is reserved for—and only for—your primary partner. This is a barrier that many couples find even more sacred than sexual monogamy.

• *Mental monogamy.* I have alluded to this earlier in the book. Mental monogamy exists when there is no attraction to anyone outside the relationship, even in your thoughts. Although it is rare that someone in the privacy of his or her own mind is exclusively committed to one partner, people often expect more of their partners than they do of themselves. (In other words: "It's okay for *me* to fantasize an outside relationship—but not okay for *you*.")

• *Serial monogamy* is an arrangement that exists between partners in a short-term or uncommitted relationship. This has become a rather popular arrangement for those in transitional relationships in the era of AIDS and several other sexually transmitted diseases that can have grave consequences. Many couples and individuals who are engaged in serial monogamy would probably have had little trouble with the idea of having multiple sex partners in the pre-AIDS era. Others, however, see no connection between their monogamous values and those ever present health risks, and would only consider having as a sexual partner someone with whom they believe exclusivity—at least for the time being—exists.

WHY MONOGAMY?

Monogamy, at its best, is predicated on the idea that you are interested only in one partner for your sexual, emotional, and intimate needs. In other words, given the infinite number of choices that are presented to you with each day, week, month, or year, you come back to your partner by choice. If this characterizes your relationship, I'd certainly say you have something worth cherishing and keeping intact. Partners who are able to maintain this level of monogamy achieve what many would say is one of the ultimate goals of a relationship. As Lewis said:

This is my third marriage. If you had asked me ten years ago what monogamy was, I would either have said a board game about Atlantic City or a type of wood. But now, for the first time, I have absolutely no desire to go elsewhere. In my two previous marriages, I had intended to stay faithful but always found myself drawn to other women. In the five years that I have been married to Cindy, I've realized that there wasn't something wrong with me, which I previously thought, but there was something very wrong with the relationships I was in. Both of my wives were faithful to me, so I don't fault them. There was just always something missing that I had to go outside of the relationship for. Now that that's no longer the case, I consider myself a lucky man.

It goes without saying that for Lewis and Cindy monogamy works. However, not everyone I ask points to happiness with their partners as the main motivator. Some other common reasons for monogamy include:

• Religious and moral values—the idea that by carrying out your desires to stray outside your marriage or primary relationship, you will receive some form of divine punishment.
• The fear of being caught.
• Your own feelings of guilt.
• The fear of AIDS or some other sexually transmitted disease.
• To keep up your end of a commitment you have made to be honest with your partner. (In this case, you place a value on honesty, even though monogamy may or may not be something you value.)

A monogamous lifestyle is certainly chosen by many (if not most) couples—regardless of the reasons.

ALTERNATIVES TO MONOGAMY

We hold monogamy in high esteem; however, on closer examination, it's evident that many couples in our society are not really monogamous. In what may be one of the most prevalent yet least talked about hypocrisies that we harbor, the prevalence of extramarital sex is quite high. Kinsey's early study showed that approximately 50 percent of all married men and 26 percent of all married women engaged in extramarital sex at least one time during their marriage.

Other more recent studies have shown that the percentage of married men who engage in extramarital sex ranges from 20 to 66 percent, and the percentage of married women having extramarital sex ranges between 20 and 69 percent. The reason that there is so much variation in the results of these studies is because of differing research methods and sampling techniques used in the surveys. I do not pretend to know the exact answer as to just how prevalent extramarital sex is, but I can certainly say that it is an issue to be understood and reckoned with.

Whether or not extramarital sex is an issue in your relationship, it is important to understand what may arise when one partner or the other does not fully subscribe to monogamy. The main alternatives to monogamy are:

- *The undisclosed affair.* This could be a one-night stand or a relationship that continues outside of your primary one for many years. A secret affair is probably the most common alternative to monogamy, even though monogamy is the *stated* arrangement between the partners.
- *Unspoken synogamy.* Sometimes there is an "understanding"—usually unspoken (or rarely spoken about)—between the partners that one or both partners may do what he or she feels it is necessary to do in order to fulfill his or her sexual and emotional needs. Although one or both partners may assume that they have the freedom to go outside of the relationship, what this *actually entails* is not discussed.
- *Synogamous arrangements.* There is a verbal agreement that one or both partners may go outside of the relationship, to varying degrees, *with* each other's knowledge.

Synogamy is a word that I coined that simply means a relationship that is not monogamous. In the next section of this chapter, we will deal with affairs that occur in relationships that are stated to be monogamous (although they are in fact synogamous). How can you and your partner heal from an affair that may have ended? What are some of the other implications of secret affairs?

THE UNDISCLOSED AFFAIR

Many people involved in undisclosed affairs go to extraordinary lengths to keep their liaisons secret. However, as we all know, this effort is not always successful. Not unlike relationships themselves, undisclosed affairs also come in many varieties:

• *Sexual liaisons.* These could be one-night stands or ongoing rendezvous that are in reality a series of trysts. Sexual liaisons can be physical affairs that don't necessarily have to include intercourse (and many of them don't in the era of AIDS). But they are grounded in excitement, based on the type of passion that is either lacking or different from that in your primary relationship.

There are risk factors in such affairs: unwanted emotional attachments; an unwanted pregnancy; or exposure to venereal disease. An undisclosed or secret affair is more likely to be seen as a harmless interlude that has little to do with anything that takes place either before or after. The emphasis in a sexual liaison is usually the *activity* that is taking place, rather than the other person.

• *Emotional affairs.* These may include sex, but often do not. Partners having an emotional affair are likely to be turning to each other because they feel a void in their primary relationships. Emotional affairs are grounded both in passion and comfort, and have much more potential than sexual liaisons to develop into relationships that challenge the security of the primary relationships. As in sexual liaisons, either partner has a potential to become more involved than the other, especially if one partner does not have a primary relationship (see Chapter 7). An emotional affair differs from a sexual liaison mainly because the emphasis is more on the *relationship between the specific two people* involved as opposed to the activities they pursue when they are together.

• *Parallel relationships.* These are usually long-term, ongoing relationships that run parallel to your primary one. Typically, a parallel relationship provides a constant source of passion, where the primary relationship provides mainly comfort. Parallel relationships can be of the variety we discussed in Chapter 7, where one partner wants it to develop into something much more, or they can exist in a situation where both are involved with other primary partners and like what they have together just fine.

There are many documented cases of presidents and other prominent people who have had parallel relationships for years. As unlikely as it may seem, many have managed to keep these relationships secret for decades. What makes a parallel relationship different from the other two types is that most who have them consider their parallel relationship to be a long-term arrangement designed as an ongoing solution to fill a large gap that exists in their primary relationship.

Although there are many who will not make a distinction in terms of what implication the above types of undisclosed affairs may have on one's primary relationship, in reality these are all quite different.

Comparing an Affair with Your Primary Relationship

I can see no better application for the cliché/metaphor of "apples versus oranges" than comparing an affair with your primary relationship. Affairs generally take place under ideal or even artificial circumstances. And for this reason, they represent one of the most common emotional illusions. Rarely will a marriage or other primary relationship compare favorably in intensity with the kinds of feelings you may have when you have a sexual or emotional liaison with someone else. When you're with that other person, you can put aside all the pressures of day-to-day living—the children, the bills, work schedules, and other realities of life—and concentrate mainly on your mutual pleasure. Let's face it, if you are tired or not feeling too well, you'll probably opt to go home and be with your spouse or primary partner. A paramour usually gets you only on "the good days" and under ideal circumstances. Affairs can go on for quite some time and still feel like they are fueled by that delicious initial attraction. That's why it is often so sad to see people hastily leave workable long-term relationships because they feel as though they have "fallen in love" with someone else—only to find out that they were merely infatuated.

If you have had this experience, perhaps you noticed that instead of familiarity breeding deeper, more positive feelings, a relationship that stemmed from an outside affair only produced disappointment when you left the primary relationship behind. Many who leave their primary relationship find this out after it is too late to go back. Unfortunately, it is often impossible to save the first relationship by ending the second. When reality sets in, however, many find that they want to end the secondary relationship as well—and as soon as possible.

Some Reasons for Having Undisclosed Affairs

There is no single set of circumstances that induces people to have affairs. The following reasons are among those I have heard recently:

- "My sex life at home just wasn't making it."
- "I had a platonic friendship with him for years and it just got out of hand. I guess you could say we became curious."
- "I just wanted to. At the time I thought that I was justified. I guess I nitpicked my marriage, and my nitpicking finally convinced me there was something wrong. After that, I easily rationalized my choice."

- "My husband and I weren't communicating and the opportunity just presented itself. I had neither the desire nor the strength to walk away."
- "We were old flames from high school and met again in a different era. So we could explore something we never had the chance to back when we actually parted virgins."
- "I guess there is something to that seven-year-itch phenomenon, although for me it was nine years."
- "My wife used to tell me if I wanted more sex I should go have an affair. One day I did."
- "I believe that the only way I can stay in a marriage that I don't want to leave, but which doesn't totally fulfill me, is to go outside to get my needs fulfilled."
- "I was just not feeling attractive in my marriage, and I needed some confirmation."
- "My husband is unable to perform, but I am still committed to him and don't want to leave the marriage."
- "For fun and lust!"
- "Although I admit I enjoyed it while it lasted, in reality it was probably to get even with my husband: He had an affair first, before I did."
- "I am a hopeless romantic and when I get that feeling, I just go with it."
- "I travel a lot and get lonely. Occasionally someone meets my fancy, and the temptation carries me away."
- "I felt more love for this person than I ever did for my partner. I needed to play it out so I could go back to my marriage."
- "I met someone for whom I feel a great deal of love. I think my marriage is over."
- "I don't think there is anything wrong with it, if both people are willing, as long as no one gets hurt."
- "I did it and found myself overcome with guilt, but at the time, guilt was the furthest thing from my mind."

If you are currently having an affair, understand what your reasons are. The statements above were made by actual people in your situation. It's possible that you can identify with many of them. If you do, then there may be some questions that you need to ask yourself. For example:

- Are you burned out—sexually or otherwise—in your primary relationship?
- Does the affair make going home to your primary relationship seem more desirable?
- Are you considering leaving your partner because you are comparing the feelings that you are experiencing toward your part-time lover with the feelings you have toward your spouse? (If this is the case, you may want to consider the implications in Chapter 7 of Prebound/Rebound Relationships.)
- Are you willing to work on putting some sorely needed passion back into your primary relationship?
- Are you acting out of some unresolved anger toward your spouse or primary partner?

If you are involved in a secret affair that you are unwilling to end, then I will have more to say about your situation later in this chapter. However, your choice may be to end the affair. If this is the case, a dilemma you may be facing is whether to tell your primary partner that the affair has taken place. Most experts agree—and experience has certainly taught me this—*that telling your partner is usually not something that benefits either of you.* Perhaps you feel guilt or shame, or perhaps you actually feel justified. It is even possible that you have all of these feelings at the same time. Some opt to tell their primary partner, as a means of clearing the air, only to find that the disclosure prompts their partner to insist that the relationship is over and that one of them must now leave. Others disclose out of a need—conscious or unconscious—to hurt their partners further. I will have more to say later in this chapter about how to help heal the situation if your affair is discovered by your partner. However, if the affair has not been discovered, then perhaps your secret affair should be the one *exception* to that rule of relationships that encourages disclosure as a means of breeding more intimacy. *Bottom line:* If you are or have been involved in an affair, *unless there is a need for your partner to know* (such as the inevitability of your paramour or someone else telling your partner, or if there is a health-related reason), *this is best kept secret.*

Is Your Partner Having an Affair?

Many people dwell on this question and, as I pointed out in the last chapter, the result is sometimes a self-fulfilling prophecy. However, if it is uncharacteristic of you to be suspicious and you have that concern, consider what are some of the most common warning signals that this may be the case:

• Has your partner recently stopped approaching you sexually? If so, is this change uncharacteristic for him or her? Have you discussed this and been able to come up with some perspective on it?

• Have there been unexplained scheduling changes? Has your partner begun to pay more attention to how he or she looks when going out—"alone"? Has he or she become more mysterious about the use of time? Has there been money spent that is unaccounted for in an uncharacteristic manner? Have there been strange calls on the phone bill or mysterious "wrong numbers"?

None of these things together or individually means anything conclusive, but they are certainly worth discussing. Rarely are people who truly do not want to be caught actually caught having an affair by their partners. It is possible to carry one on for years and years without leaving any tangible signs. Lipstick left on collars, motel bills, and being seen by one's mother-in-law in a compromising situation make much better fiction and drama than reality.

But if you notice your partner becoming more and more distant, yes, it could be a sign that there is an affair going on; or it could be any one of a number of other issues. If there is ever something not to procrastinate over, it's bringing your dissatisfaction with your partner's distance to his or her attention. If these issues are not dealt with, the result is not inevitably an affair, but it can certainly be the beginning of the end of your relationship for many possible reasons. There is no shortcut to good communication. It's always discouraging when I hear couples talk about early warning signs that could have been easily worked on at the time, but were ignored to the point where reversing them has become extremely difficult or impossible.

Normally, you will not discover that your partner has had an affair unless he or she tells you, or you learn about it by some fluke, or if your partner sets himself or herself up to be caught. The latter can happen either consciously or unconsciously.

If You Have Discovered (or Been Told) Your Partner Has Had an Affair

Suppose you do find out that your partner has had an affair:

• Does this mean that your relationship is now doomed? No, not unless either one of you decides that is the case.
• Do you now have something to hold over his or her head as long as you both shall live? Only if you want a miserable existence until your relationship does finally, and inevitably, end.
• Is this something that you can ever forget? Forget, well hardly; forgive, absolutely! In fact, it is very important that if you decide that your relationship is worth saving that you do work it out and *then forgive your partner because that is the only true road to healing in this case.*

Here is what some people who have been in your shoes have said about the realization that their partner has had an affair:

• "I have never been more devastated in my life."
• "I hate to admit it, but while it was going on I felt almost off the hook. Now that I look back at it, it was an eerie but comfortable feeling."

- "What am I missing? What have I done to contribute to this?"
- "We better both get tested to see if we have any diseases."
- "I can't believe that someone with whom I have shared so much could do this to me."
- "I can live with the affair—it's the lies that I can't handle."
- "Now I know how my wife felt when she found out that I was having one."
- "I will never be able to trust him again."

As these reactions show, people's reactions range from near indifference to near devastation. It may pay you to do some soul-searching at this point. If you want your relationship to continue, it is most important to determine what you need to do in order to begin to rebuild trust with your partner. But before we get to your partner, here are a few things that you may want to keep in mind:

- Ask yourself what signs you ignored and what, if anything, may have been your payoff in ignoring those signs. As one person said: "I felt as though I was off the hook as long as I believed my partner wasn't having an affair." Were you off the hook to some degree? If so, are you willing to look at the possibility that you wanted to deny the situation? Denial may have served you in some very beneficial ways.
- Try to focus on the real thing. Don't be concerned about things such as, what did the other man or woman look like?; how do I compare with him or her? etc., etc. The only thing you may have against that other person is that you both have similar tastes when it comes to your partner. Unless you also feel betrayed by someone (a friend or family member) close to you, your partner is the only person with whom you have an issue to be resolved.
- If you have discovered or been told about an almost forgotten affair that took place and ended long ago, the threat that you feel about this may be very overexaggerated. Long-past affairs are generally easier to forgive. Yet a surprising

number of relationships that have worked very well since the affair took place break up because there is not awareness that such an event can be forgiven.

Toward Healing

To heal after an affair has taken place, consider the following:

• Talk with your partner about why it happened and try to see his/her point of view.

• Determine what it is that you need from your partner to forgive him or her, and ask for that. It could be a promise, an explanation, or a commitment to work out the anger in therapy. Whatever it is, try to lay that all on the table.

• There is no ironclad guarantee that it will never happen again. Although some suspicion is probably normal afterwards, don't make your partner pay for it for the rest of his or her life.

• Getting over this is almost like a grieving process, which could take as long as a year or sometimes even longer. Accept that things may not be right for a while.

• You may not in fact be as angry as you thought you would be. If this is the case, consider it a bonus, not a sign that you care less for your partner than you thought you did.

• It is true that the best predictor of future behavior is past behavior, but that self-fulfilling prophecy principle can work more than once. By making it too difficult for healing to take place between you and your partner, you could in effect be sending your partner right back into the arms of the person from whom he or she has just broken up.

• If there is ever anything that should be kept as a private matter between the two of you, it is the disclosure of an affair. In-laws sometimes have much more trouble forgiving than partners do.

• Trust is built once again by working through some of the particulars. Why did the affair happen? Was it out of boredom, anger, dissatisfaction at home? Was there just a blinding lust? Was it a casual fling—or an affair with heavy emotional involvement? Did it happen during a time when there was some crisis going on—when having an affair seemed like a kind of escape? Are you willing to share some of the blame for letting the relationship deteriorate, if that is what happened? How much harm has really been done? If it is all over and you are considering splitting up, is splitting up really what you want—or is it an overreaction, a kind of punishment? (If so, remember you may wind up being punished just as much or more than the partner you're trying to punish.)

• Have you each learned something by this experience? (How sad it would be if this much pain did not yield some learning.)

• At first, it is normal to feel hurt, anger, and even hate. But forgiving begins when you start to see the situation in a new light. Once you have forgiven, *let it go.* If it comes up again in your thoughts, don't reblame that occurrence on your partner once you have forgiven.

A relationship does not have to end merely because one partner has had an affair. However, it is essential to establish trust once again. The good news is that a relationship that survives this could actually be a relationship that is stronger than either of you could ever have imagined.

In the next section we will talk about relationships that may even need synogamy to survive.

UNSPOKEN SYNOGAMY

Unspoken synogamous agreements are similar to secret affairs in that generally the fact that one or both partners will not be monogamous is implicitly accepted. However, that acceptance usually breaks down very quickly if the synogamous partner's activities are discovered. When this discovery is made, there can be just as much of a crisis as with the secret affair. But there is a difference. In this case, the offense usually is not so much what the synogamous partner has done, but the fact that it has been discovered—and therefore the issue must be confronted. In other words, this is an arrangement where the unspoken rule is, "Do what you please, but don't let me find out"; or, "You are going to do whatever it is that you want to do anyway, but be discreet and don't cause us embarrassment, get any diseases, or do anything else that will hurt our comfortable lifestyle."

Unspoken synogamy is common in marriages where sex has for one reason or another stopped being a part of the relationship. Reasons for this could include:

• A medical or physical reason that prevents one partner from being sexually available to the other.

• There is the lack of desire between partners to have sex with each other. Partners then adopt the attitude that almost anything would be better than being repeatedly resentful or faced with indifference. Thus, the ongoing tension around the issue of sex quietly disappears.

• Some couples have grown apart sexually to such a degree that perhaps they even have different sexual orientations. Although enough remains in the relationship to keep them together, the sexual attraction is elsewhere.

• Some couples have an unspoken understanding that when one or both partners is away, it is likely, and therefore okay, that some indiscretion can occur. The attitude usually is, "Who will know anyway?" or, "It's not that big a deal." A similar attitude is, "As long as it is a one-night stand, this infidelity does not need to affect our lives." This can be called a tryst with a twist, for usually couples who adopt this arrangement know each other well enough to trust that there is little likelihood of emotional attachment. As one couple amusingly described it: "Since we met at a professional convention, we both sort of give each other 'convention privileges.' We don't ask questions, we don't check up on each other, and, ironically, we don't feel threatened about it either."

A more common type of unspoken agreement is the kind where one or both partners have a parallel relationship:

George was fifty-two when he came into therapy and complained about feelings of guilt related to a parallel relationship he had been having for over a year with Karen, a thirty-four-year-old professional woman. Like many in his dilemma, George was not willing to give up either his marriage or this intensely passionate extramarital romance. For George, the most uncomfortable aspect of his double life was the deception. In fact, he cared for his wife Alice deeply. They had three grown children and had been married for almost thirty years. George and Alice enjoyed a very affluent lifestyle together: He was in a top management position. Alice's support was essential to his success story. The only thing that seemed to be missing in their lifestyle, for George, was sexual fulfillment. Alice admittedly had a low sex drive and usually was sexual with George only in order to accommodate him. George had had many sexual liaisons over the years—mainly with prostitutes—but never with anyone who meant something to him, as Karen did.

In summary, here was the problem: George had a comfortable and, on many important levels, fulfilling marriage to Alice, which he is unwilling to give up. He had a passionate, ongoing, sexual and emotional affair with Karen, which he was equally unwilling to give up. ("She makes life really worth living in a way that I have never felt before," he said repeatedly.) The situation triggered enormous feelings of guilt for George. At my suggestion, he first brought in Karen. She admitted, both in front of George and alone, that she would not be in favor of him leaving his wife. "I could never be responsible for fulfilling all of George's needs. When he is with me, it's great, but I am not willing to make a commitment to someone eighteen years older than me. When I settle down, it will be with someone closer to my age so we'll have similar ideas about starting a family. George has three grown children. I have never met them and have no desire to. In addition, I want to be free to see other people. It's possible that George and I will go on forever, but if that's the case, this is as far as I want it to go. When George leaves to go back to his wife, I feel fulfilled and almost never sorry to see him go."

George echoed that if he did have to choose between Karen and Alice, he would go back to Alice, but this would not be a choice that he would initiate. In a subsequent session, George brought in Alice, who did not know about his relationship with

Karen. Alice was everything George said she was. She was a witty and intelligent woman who understood George quite well. They had built a fine life together, and both felt very secure in it. Alice admitted that there had been a problem throughout their marriage with her sexual desire. She acknowledged it as a problem, however, only to the extent that it bothered George. Privately, she denied ever having any type of affair outside of the relationship, and did so in a way that I had no trouble at all believing her.

With George in the room, however, what she articulated was exactly what George needed to hear to absolve him of his guilt. Alice said, "I used to feel very guilty about either turning George down sexually or going along with the program just to satisfy him. But for the past year or so, I guess George's sex drive became more similar to mine. We have sex now about once a month—maybe less—and that's about all George wants it to be. For me, that has been enough for many years. For a while I thought George was having an affair, but then I realized: What difference would it make as long as nothing changed in our relationship and we were able to stay together? That is really *all* that's important."

In the next session, George came by himself. He realized that all three players—Alice, Karen, and himself—in fact had what they wanted. He was able to let go of his guilt and, to my knowledge, this arrangement still continues.

If George's case is atypical at all, it is only in that Alice was able to verbalize what many people in her situation accept silently. George, like many of us, believed in monogamy intellectually, but was unable to happily live that lifestyle. His case illustrates how synogamy kept a "monogamous" marriage together. George's lifestyle has always been common. However, in recent years both the news media and an array of memoirs have made us aware of many prominent people—politicians, business and religious leaders, as well as other celebrities— who presently or in the past, conduct their private lives in this manner.

SYNOGAMOUS ARRANGEMENTS

Some individuals recognize and accept their inability or unwillingness to maintain monogamy within their relationship.

In some cases, neither partner is willing to agree to exclusivity. Some of the more common "designer arrangements" of such couples include:

• *Open marriage.* This is a concept that was first described by Nena and George O'Neill in their 1972 best-seller, *Open Marriage.* An arrangement of open marriage essentially gives each partner the option of pursuing others outside the relationship for any purpose that cannot be fulfilled within the relationship—including, but not necessarily, sex. The idea behind a couple having this degree of freedom was that each partner would bring positive feelings acquired elsewhere back into the relationship. The one major ground rule, of course, was that an outside relationship would not preempt or become more important than the primary relationship. I have known several couples (but not many) who have successfully been able to pull this off.

Open marriages that work are, in fact, rare. In my experience, there has got to be a good relationship to begin with for it to even have a chance. In other words, it is not a concept that I have ever seen to be an effective remedy for a troubled relationship. But those few couples with long-standing open marriages do seem to have better than average relationships, and enthusiastically embrace the concept.

• *Group marriage.* This concept was popular in the late sixties and seventies, and usually had ground rules that included some degree of monogamy, but with a twist: Sexual activities would be confined to members who shared a group living arrangement. This could include two, three, or even more couples. In some cases, the arrangement was merely a ménage à trois. Only on rare occasions have I seen this type of arrangement work for more than a few years. Typically, couples pair off—not necessarily with the partner they started out with—and go their separate ways. Group marriages often, but not necessarily, involve some degree of bisexual activity as well.

• *Swinging and group sex.* In this arrangement, sex outside the marriage is usually done with each other's close supervision and watchful eye. Swingers find partners in several ways:

They advertise in certain specialty publications, go to events and establishments known to cater to swingers, or find their counterparts by word of mouth. Couples typically attend the events together, but then partners go off by themselves, exchange partners, or sometimes engage in group sexual activities.

It goes without saying that this practice can pose many health threats, yet it is still a common fringe practice. A major drawback has always been that few couples become interested in swinging in a mutual way. More typically, it is one partner who initiates the idea. In order to get the other partner to agree to go to these "couples only" activities, the enthusiastic partner often has to convince the reluctant partner to go. In an effort to save the relationship or to appease the enthusiastic partner, the reluctant one will give it a try. However, many couples are not ready for the emotional consequences such as jealousy, and sometimes humiliation, that often accompany swinging, and they sometimes find themselves in an unexpected and perhaps irreparable crisis. On balance, some research has actually shown that many couples who engage in swinging rate their relationships as happier and more fulfilling. It is questionable, however, whether this is because of, unrelated to, or in spite of, their swinging activities.

> ## ADDITIONAL PERSPECTIVES ON SYNOGAMY

Undoubtedly, there are readers who would find a section on synogamy more suitable for a book about why and how relationships break up than for one about how to keep them together. And, indeed, it would have been easy to leave much of this chapter out. But, in my opinion, to do so would only help perpetuate an all-too-common hypocrisy—that these synogamous marriages just don't exist in "normal" society. Indeed, studies and statistics show otherwise. Synogamy in all its forms is prevalent. In my experience, many need help coming to grips with what synogamy might imply if, in fact, their own relationships depend on this kind of arrangement. In that regard, be aware of the following:

• Not everyone can be happily monogamous. It is just as reasonable to expect that both partners will not remain monogamous throughout a long-term relationship as to expect that they will. Therefore, it is important for you to understand the realities so that if this comes up in your relationship, you know that *there are alternatives apart from your relationship automatically ending.*

• The primary relationship and an affair are distinctly different. They are not comparable, and experience has shown that one does not necessarily lead to the other. A person outside has a lot going for him or her that can make that person appear to be more attractive and passionate than your primary partner. *Don't get carried away by this illusion.*

• Those couples who have been able to have successful synogamous arrangements have invariably done so because they have put their primary partner first and kept their primary partner first. Synogamy is rarely an effective substitute for facing the issues in your relationship.

• *No responsible discussion of synogamy would be complete without mentioning the health hazards in this day of AIDS and other extremely serious sexually transmitted diseases.* The only absolutely safe sex is monogamous sex with a partner who has never had the opportunity to become infected by anyone else.

Methods for safer sex are well known and should be religiously observed if you are engaging in any kind of sexual activity that puts you or your partner at risk. During the sexual revolution, the conventional wisdom was, "Listen to your body." Now, more than ever, your brain has to participate as well. Never engage in sexual activity with someone who is unwilling to share your concerns about the possibility that what you hope will be a harmless activity could become a death sentence. *In reality, no matter what is said, ultimately your comfort level will prevail, but err on the side of caution.*

As I said earlier, there are many who engage in synogamous lifestyles. However, there are many who don't. In presenting this topic, my goal, as always, is to help you to understand your choices—not to moralize. Know what works for you, and think in terms of *long-range consequences,* for yourself and your partner.

CHAPTER ELEVEN

THE CASE FOR AND AGAINST PARENTHOOD

For many couples, deciding whether or not to have children can be an unexpectedly painful and complex choice. Arguably, it is the most important decision that you and your partner will ever make. Indeed, many good relationships have turned sour over this question. For many, the panic to have a child has even brought them into relationships that they otherwise would hardly have considered if the urgency to be a parent were not at the forefront.

Back in the days when men and women assumed that they would have children soon after they were married, having children was not such an issue. People generally got married at a younger age, and the children came soon after. The man developed his career, while his wife generally had primary responsibility for raising the children. Very few couples discussed other alternatives—such as having children much later, or not having them at all.

Then times changed. Marrying later seemed, for many, like a more prudent thing to do. "I'll develop my career first," people told themselves. "Then I'll get to see the world." It was assumed that the decision to get married would be a more educated choice, since those who married later had a greater degree of maturity. But, for many, just at the point when they thought having children would finally seem natural, some new questions emerged: Who would interrupt his or her career to take care of the children? "Is having kids something I (or we) really want to do?" "Do we really want to give up so much we enjoy just at the point when we've become thoroughly convinced we can have it all?"

Since there was no clear direction, many couples wondered whether they could put it off for a while. But what about that biological clock?

Since, in reality, there is only a limited period of time when women can safely conceive, the time limit is a pressure on many couples. Conflicts arise—either between you and your partner or within yourself. Often those conflicts are between what makes sense on paper and what your deepest emotions tell you. What do you need for fulfillment in your life? How does one resolve a conflict between maternal instinct and the freedom that comes with not having children? If you continue your career and lifestyle, will you someday wish you had sacrificed some of both in order to have children?

> ## THE MOST IMPORTANT DECISION YOU MAY EVER MAKE

If you thought marrying or making a commitment to your partner was the most important decision you could make, consider what most divorce lawyers will tell you: *It is not whom you marry, it is whom you have children with.* Unworkable marriages without children can still be profoundly difficult to end, but once healing has occurred, you can usually make a clean break. With a child in the picture, like it or not, on some level you will always be married "till death do you part." So the first, and perhaps most important, thing for you to consider is whether you are bringing a child into a strong enough relationship.

Each partner's desires are extremely important. I believe that if either of you is not in favor of having a child, the prudent course is to give yourselves as much time as you possibly can to clear up your ambivalence before taking this step. Due to the irreversible nature of this decision, many couples in their twenties and early thirties are considering very deliberately the question of whether to have children. Many feel they need more time to reach greater certainty about their life goals. So while there are no pat answers, here are some criteria for you and your partner to consider to help you to find the answer that works for you:

THE CASE FOR PARENTHOOD

If you and your partner enjoy children, having your own can be intrinsically rewarding on many levels:

• Fulfillment of your parental instincts—both maternal and paternal. The reality is that being a parent gives you access to a bond that probably cannot be duplicated in any other form of relationship. The experience of parenthood is an emotional one that allows you to live, love, and give in a way that is unique.

• You have the opportunity to procreate and to continue your genealogy. In a sense, a part of you can remain alive long after you are materially gone from this earth.

• Having children can, of course, lead to grandchildren and the pleasure of having the companionship of adult children later on in life.

• Being parents together can also develop an additional bond between you and your partner.

If you obtain most of your gratification outside of yourself, child-rearing is an exercise—perhaps the ultimate exercise—in delayed gratification. In addition, being a parent can provide you with the enormous gratification of seeing the world through a child's eyes once again. However, those for whom the life-style of a parent works best are those who neither demand nor expect the lion's share of that immense pleasure that being a parent can provide to come from anywhere except from within themselves.

THE CASE AGAINST PARENTHOOD

Since this is one of the few decisions in life that is usually irrevocable, I urge you to err on the side of caution. If you have never had children, just imagine the effort that it takes to raise one. While imagining this, really exaggerate the task at hand, and then multiply it by four (some would say ten). That's about how much effort it actually does take. It is not hard to see how parenthood, without the intrinsic rewards, can be—as many have described it—a tortuous experience.

Consider the following points to be an obstacle course. Get through it, and the reward will be some much-needed clarity on this issue.

• Parenthood will change every aspect of your present life-style (for example, you will have less control over when you eat, sleep, and even shower).

• It will account for much of (if not all of) your spare time. If you are not ready for this to happen, then this is probably not the time.

• An often-perpetuated myth is that having children will save or improve a bad or unfulfilling marriage. Nothing can be further from the truth. Children often strain and test the endurance of even the best marriages. To give your life meaning, make you feel more worthwhile, or to provide an object in your life that will provide *you* with love, are not reasons to have a child either. After all, isn't that putting a lot of pressure on an unborn person? The best parents are those who would feel worthwhile whether they are parents or not.

Here are some additional considerations that should probably not be factors in your decision to have children:

• Because you believe that it's a stigma to go through life without children.

• Because you want to give your parents grandchildren.

• You wish to avoid the label of seeming "selfish." Of course I would counter, isn't it even more selfish to bring a child into the world for the wrong reasons—if that child may in reality be unwanted?

• Because you are panicking. If you are a woman, you may feel that your biological clock is getting dangerously close to midnight. Choices in any area of life that are made solely as a reaction to panic are subject to an inordinate degree of error.

Certainly you are capable of evaluating for yourself whether a child of yours would be wanted or unwanted. If you can truly say to your partner, "I want to care for a child with you"— and if your partner feels the same way—then in all likelihood having a child will be a choice you won't regret.

TOWARD RESOLVING THE DILEMMA

Don't be surprised if exploring this issue taps some of the deepest roots of your personal value system; the very foundation of your partner's value system; and the very foundation of your relationship. The following examples illustrate some of the issues that can arise:

• Janet has always been ambivalent about having children. Her husband Seth, however, never wanted children at all, and often refused to even discuss it. Seth's behavior, coupled with Janet's ambivalence, made them postpone the decision longer and longer, until Janet reached the point in life when it was too late for her. This suddenly generated an unprecedented amount of anger and resentment toward Seth, which nearly broke up their marriage.

• Eileen and Paul's marriage was in a critical phase when they entered counseling. They had always assumed they would have children, but kept postponing their decision so that they could take care of other priorities first. Those priorities included extensive travel on vacations; allowing Eileen to finish graduate school; and allowing time for the couple to become more financially stable. Eileen was about thirty-five when she became pregnant.

Of course, Eileen and Paul's lives were never the same again once the baby was born. Eileen—once quite content in her marriage—now complained that Paul was selfish and unwilling to help with the chores and responsibilities that came with having a child. She complained that while his career hadn't skipped a beat, hers had to be put on hold. Paul complained that since the baby had arrived, Eileen seemed to have forgotten that he was alive. Their sex life deteriorated, and they had very little fun. He admitted even being jealous of the baby at times.

Both admitted, with a bit of reservation and a tremendous amount of guilt, that their new baby had put much more of a strain on the marriage and their lifestyle than they could ever have imagined. At the same time, they both grumbled that the amount of joy they experienced was not nearly enough to make it worthwhile. Their marriage is still intact, but the issues that Eileen and Paul need to address are ongoing.

• Clara and Dick had considered having children several times during their ten-year marriage. As both of them approached forty, they realized that they were unwilling to give up the lifestyle they had created for themselves. Although they sometimes had twinges of regret, both knew that, all things considered, they had made the right decision. Thus, for Clara and Dick the feelings that occasionally made them consider having children were not nearly strong enough to be acted upon.

• Allen and Jane married in their late twenties. For the first several years of their marriage, they agreed that they might never want children. Like many of their contemporaries, they were mostly involved with developing their own careers. Then, slowly, Jane began to feel the desire to become a mother. Allen was at first ambivalent and skeptical, but then became quite supportive of Jane. They realized that all the things they wanted to do with their lives did not really conflict with becoming parents. After much thought, and after considering the idea of parenthood over some time, Jane became pregnant. Four years later, the couple had a second child. When asked how their new way of life had evolved, they simply said, "We grew up." Both Jane and Allen felt that having children was, for them, the right choice.

• Jennifer's first marriage broke up mainly because she was against the idea of parenthood in her twenties and early thirties. During most of her late thirties, she was single and unattached. At times, she felt strongly that she wanted to become a mother; but the "urge" would often pass for a while after she spent time with friend's children (of various ages). Later, she became involved with and married Ken, whose children from his first marriage lived with him. Jennifer was able to have what she described as "the best of all possible worlds" by becoming a stepmother to Ken's children.

• Nancy and Sid started their marriage with an agreement that they would not have children. Nancy was in her early twenties—and undecided. Sid, however, was adamant that he did not want children under any circumstances. About ten years into the marriage, they began fighting about Nancy's urge to become a mother. Sid, however, was adamant that he wanted no part of parenthood. One day Nancy admitted that she had been a little lax with birth control (although she was not pregnant). Sid immediately, and without her knowing beforehand, went to get a vasectomy. Within six months, they were divorced.

Each of these couples presents a complex story. All had fairly good relationships when the issue of parenthood challenged them. For each, the outcome was different, yet all felt it was the most critical decision of their marriage. I would have to echo this and add that I would be at a loss to identify a normal issue that could possibly be more critical.

SOME LITMUS TEST QUESTIONS

The following are some questions that I strongly urge you to discuss with your partner as you determine whether parenthood is in the cards for you:

- Why do you really want children?
- Are you ready to make parenting your top priority?
- Can your relationship withstand the realities of you and your partner having less private time together when the two of you are alone and relaxed? For example, your new lifestyle may preclude those two- and three-week vacations you enjoy together, as well as some lazy weekends with little responsibility that may be part of your current lifestyle. For some relationships, parenthood will mean spending more time together, in others less. How does that prospect feel?
- What sacrifices specifically need to be made? Career sacrifices? Money sacrifices? Will you have to give up a living space that suited you as a couple—but may not be suitable for a family with children?
- Do you and your partner like being with babies? Small children? Older children? Adolescents? Do you trust your temperament, especially your level of patience?
- If you want to be a parent now, be sure to calculate how old you will be when your child is ten, fifteen, and twenty. Are you comfortable visualizing yourself as a parent at those later stages?
- Is your vision of parenthood doing hands-on parenting yourself? Or are you expecting your partner to take care of the child or children? Do you intend to have other help, hired or otherwise?
- How many children do you now believe that you ultimately want? Over what period of time?
- Will you settle for a boy or a girl? Or does your enthusi-

asm change depending upon the sex or other characteristics of the baby?

• If you were unable to have kids, or chose not to have them, would you still relish your relationship with your partner? Or are you looking at parenthood as a means to give your relationship a "shot in the arm"?

These questions are designed to help you and your partner be open with each other on the deepest possible level. I urge you to do this without any interference from others, such as parents, who probably have their own biases. As you discuss this subject, I hope you will be able to listen to each other's point of view without trying to coerce your partner into seeing things your way.

WHEN ONE OF YOU DOESN'T WANT CHILDREN . . .

How can you come to an understanding when one partner wants to have children and the other one doesn't?

When there is any ambivalence on either partner's part, I especially recommend that couples maintain an ongoing dialogue. Many couples find that one or both partners change their minds, and new ideas regarding parenthood emerge as each of you matures, both separately and as a couple. However, if you and your partner are at odds, consider the following:

• A partner who consistently tells you that he or she does not want children is to be believed.

• I have never heard of a happy scenario where one partner forced parenthood upon the other. Stopping birth control without mutual consent is more likely to lead you further apart than to "resolve" the disagreement with a fait accompli.

• To assume that your partner will change his or her mind in time is probably setting yourself up for disappointment and prolonging the problem to the point of crisis. Rather than count on a partner's "change of heart," it is better to take appropriate steps while all options are open to you. How strong is your desire to be a parent? Are you agreeable to staying in your relationship even if you don't have children? In some cases, you might want to consider ending the relationship, but also consider single-parenting options (discussed later in the chapter). Others might wish to compromise by adopting an older child or becoming foster parents.

Communication about each of your preferences and desires is essential. I think it's best to approach the subject of parenthood as early in the relationship as possible. And it's highly desirable to keep the subject open and approachable on both sides, reaching agreement in a length of time that is comfortable to you. This is the best way to safeguard against the possibility of you ultimately missing out on what could be an extremely important part of your life—being a parent.

CONCEIVE NOW OR FOREVER HOLD YOUR PEACE

Many women, because of ambivalence or the lack of opportunity, reach the end of their thirties before facing the reality that their biological ability to conceive does not have a lot of time left. The dilemma of the biological clock has never been as common as it has been in recent times. The advent of birth control pills, the proliferation of couples in which each partner has a significant career, and the popularity of the concept of zero population growth have all contributed to the prevalence of "putting off" the decision to have children. In addition, the acceptance of the single lifestyle has often put the prospect of parenthood on the back burner, until it becomes apparent that if it is to happen, it needs to happen soon. For many women, the idea of having children and making career sacrifices was out of the question until their mid-to-late thirties. Often, not having children was okay with her partner, who cannot understand why she is now changing her mind. But sometimes this change in values and desire is something from which the relationship does not recover.

Depression often sets in when it becomes apparent that, for biological reasons, it is too late to have children. Technology is pushing the age of inevitability back toward the mid-forties, and even beyond that, but it is, nonetheless, a time when factors other than choice enter into the mix. Although there is no sure-fire formula for avoiding that depression brought on by the reality that childbearing is no longer an option, you may feel more in control if you have made a conscious choice, rather than putting off your decision until it is too late.

Here are some of the other possibilities to consider regarding the end of your biological ability to bear children:

• You are in a relationship with a man who does not want children, yet you do. If you yield to his wishes, there is a good chance that once you know beyond doubt that it is too late to bear children, there will be a great deal of anger and resentment toward him. On the other hand, if you are in this situation and decide at the eleventh hour to have a child, it is also possible that you will have little paternal support. Either way, this situation, if not anticipated in time for each person to make his and her necessary choices, can jeopardize your relationship.

• You are in a relationship where your husband or partner wants children, but you do not. He pledges that he will take the more active role in caring for the baby once it is born. If this is the case, you need to determine just how much you can trust that promise and whether his playing a less active role would change your mind. If you decide reluctantly to bear a child, it is possible that you will be sorry later on. On the other hand, if you decide not to, it's possible that your partner, who does not have a biological clock (as you do), at some point will begin eyeing women who are still eligible to be mothers.

• You are unattached and truly want a child, but see no prospect of a relationship where you are willing to make a commitment to a man who will share the parenting responsibilities with you. In this situation, you can be artificially inseminated, or be impregnated by an informed father who will waive his paternal rights. This course of action has legal implications, but is not uncommon. Also, many women have chosen to become impregnated without (ever) telling the father. Only your own ethics and sense of values can determine whether these are options for you. Before making any of these choices, however, weigh the financial and emotional burdens of raising a child on your own.

• It is also quite possible to adopt a child later on, even if you are past the age when you can bear your own.

Although the biological clock is a reality, women who find that their maternal instincts have kicked in later in life can often find some way of nurturing a child—an adopted child, a niece or nephew, a "little sister or brother," or a needy older child. What is most important is that you respect both the factors within yourself and the factors in your relationship that made you wait this long. Don't try to second-guess your decision from hindsight.

INFERTILE COUPLES

For many couples, putting off having children has not been a choice. Rather, they do not have children because either or both partners are unable to conceive. This can be an equally stressful situation. Infertile couples will typically react by being surprised and shocked. Often those initial feelings turn to anger, blame toward the infertile partner, guilt, and, quite often, depression. Many experience a grief reaction; and since it is usually one person in the relationship who is responsible for the infertility, that person tends to be blamed by the other one—although often not consciously.

Working this problem out generally involves a focus on restructuring the relationship and moving beyond the crisis. This can include one or more of the following options:

• You might give up the idea of parenthood altogether, but continue to work on the feelings until they are resolved.

• Would you consider adopting a child?

• Using one or more of the methods of artificial insemination or surrogate motherhood might be options.

• For couples who have found it difficult or prohibitively expensive to adopt through normal channels, there may be other options—special foreign adoptions, adopting older children, becoming foster parents, or adopting members of special groups for whom there is less competition (such as handicapped or minority children). These have all been solutions for some people.

Only you and your partner can determine how far you are willing to go if you truly desire to have children to nurture. Before taking any definitive steps, however, it is important to resolve the blame and other negative forces that could be driving you to do something you may regret later on. Make yours a rational decision, not one that is motivated by panic or other negative emotions.

IF YOU BECOME PREGNANT NOT BY CHOICE

Couples and individuals who find themselves in this situation also have to turn to their own value systems for the answer.

Many couples who would never have considered choosing to be parents together find that once a pregnancy has occurred, and they have reevaluated the situation, being parents together begins to look like a workable situation. However, that is not a "given," and in fact for many couples it has spelled disaster.

Other options to having the child include:

• Abortion.

• Having the baby and putting it up for adoption.

• Having the child and letting someone else close to you raise it.

• Becoming a single parent.

• Obtaining counseling with your partner to explore your options in more depth—particularly if a clear decision is not made as you approach the end of the first trimester of pregnancy.

```
┌─────────────────────────────────┐
│  SOME IMPORTANT POINTS          │
│  TO REMEMBER                    │
└─────────────────────────────────┘
```

As in all complex issues, no one solution works for everyone. But here are some of the points that would be best for you and your partner to keep in the forefront of your minds:

• The decision whether or not to have a child needs to be made solely by you and your mate. Your parents may want grandchildren and be disappointed if they don't have them, but they are not *entitled* to grandchildren. Conceiving a child out of guilt is not going to serve anyone in the long run.

• Remember, there are no refunds and no exchanges! All sales are final! This is one decision you make that is irreversible and will be with you for the rest of your life. If you are still interested, read on . . .

• A baby will change virtually every aspect of your present lifestyle. It will put demands on you in ways that you have perhaps never imagined. Still, in the right circumstances, it is one of life's most rewarding experiences. But, only if you are ready, willing, and able to handle the responsibility and the drastic changes.

• Being a parent is an intrinsically rewarding experience. This means that the joy and other good feelings you get need to be *self*-generated. It's a good sign if you *know* this is something you want to do, that is, your feelings are in favor of this choice; and if anything needs to be worked out, it's the logistics.

• Reasons for *not* having a child?

- Making you feel worthwhile. (Work on your self-esteem first, then see if you are still interested.)
- To have someone to take care of you in your old age. (That's a long, long time away, with many rows to hoe in the meantime.)
- To save your marriage. (That's like having to decide whether a truck is too heavy to cross a wooden bridge, and solving the problem by loading it up with bricks.)
- To provide an escape from working; or to make your mate grow up. (If these are the main reasons driving you, do humanity a favor and adopt a pet for the time being!)

• If you are still not sure, you may want to put the decision off just a bit longer, until you can get some counseling to explore your ambivalence. It's especially important to find out whether your ambivalence is a personal issue or a function of the relationship that you are in—and the short-term intervention of a counselor can be extremely effective in helping you clarify that.

• If you have decided not to have children and found that you are sorry later on when perhaps it is too late, acknowledge those things that not having a child has *added* to your life instead of focusing on the regret. Perhaps this may include career accomplishments, the opportunity to have traveled, or to have transferred your life elsewhere. I have yet to meet someone who has everything he or she wants in life. As special an experience as parenting is, many childless people will tell you that having a child is in no way an absolute prerequisite for leading a fulfilling life.

• If you are considering having a second child, most agree that parenting does get somewhat easier after the first child, because you are more experienced and, hopefully, more mature. But, remember, having a second child is no longer "a given" anymore than is having a first one. Consider many of the same points when making that decision.

Ironically, most happy parents who at one time had reservations will tell you that if you have to question your decision, the truth is that you're probably not yet ready. It is a given that changes will occur both in your life and the nature of your relationship. After all, you will be less available to each other. You'll have less energy for your careers, and certainly less time for fun activities. (In fact, these often seem impossible during the early stages of parenthood.) But if this prospect doesn't scare you, then having a child could be one of the most meaningful aspects of your relationship and your life.

CHAPTER TWELVE

"STAYING TOGETHER FOR THE CHILDREN"

and Other Justifiable Reasons

Sandra and Barry were married for eight years. They had two children, ages four and six. Their marriage had been very much of the stormy variety. As Sandra describes it:

> We were both very controlling people. The things we fought about, as I look back, were never a big deal. It was just never the nature of either one of us to give in. At the beginning, our sex life was okay, but as time went on, we each put up walls, and eventually sex went by the wayside. About the only thing we ever seemed to be in harmony about were our children. Barry is an excellent father, and I think he would say that I'm a good mother. But at the time we decided to separate and later divorce, there was little else keeping us together besides the children.

Although I interviewed them separately, Barry pretty much echoed what Sandra said about the reason for their breakup, but added: "Except for the bonds that I felt for my children, it seemed like my only role around the house was to be that of a provider." When the couple came into counseling, I asked the question that most therapists routinely ask in such situations: "If it weren't for the kids, would you stay together?" Barry and Sandra both answered that question with what must have been at the time for them uncharacteristic agreement— that if it weren't for the children they would absolutely not be together.

The couple agreed to separate, but in the four years that they were apart, each failed to find a happier lifestyle. The children stayed with Sandra, but Barry had joint custody and unlimited visitation rights, which he eagerly took advantage of. The four of them celebrated certain holidays together, and, to the amazement of both of them, for the first time Barry and Sandra became friends. They talked to each other about people they were dating and about what Sandra and Barry both refer to as "the horrors of the single scene."

By now the children were eight and ten years old. Barry and Sandra had just turned forty, about two months apart. "I don't know who came up with the idea first," Sandra explained. "But one day we decided that maybe at this unlikely stage of our lives, we ought to try to get back together once again."

The thought of reconciliation intrigued both of them, and they decided to explore the possibility. But they also agreed not to say anything to the children unless something definite was about to happen. The couple went back into therapy to explore their move toward reconciliation. There had been no sexual contact whatsoever for a while before their initial breakup; and they both readily admitted that there was not a lot of sexual desire between them. They also admitted that they would not be taking this idea seriously if it weren't for the fact that they had two beautiful children they both wanted to be around full-time. Moreover, they believed they had matured to the point where they would not engage in the destructive dynamics of their previous married life.

On this basis, the couple were reconciled. They first agreed to live together for a year. Then they remarried. Their marriage this time is based on a high degree of comfort and a very minimal amount of passion. However, they are both much happier than they were during their four-year period of separation. They have what each of them describe as "an ironclad commitment" to stay together at least until "the children are grown."

For Barry and Sandra, learning to compromise with each other could happen only after a four-year separation. During the separation and gradual reconciliation, they learned to compromise on their expectations of what the relationship would give them.

Although they would prefer to have more passion as part of their current arrangement, they have learned to do without it in order to preserve something that they both consider— after *much* deliberation—to be more important.

John and Sonya have been married fifteen years and have three children. Although they live in the same house, they have separate bedrooms and pretty much lead their own lives. On several occasions, they seriously contemplated divorce, but would always come back to the fact that neither of them wanted to be the noncustodial parent of their children. In addition, the financial burden of divorce, and the anticipated expense of sustaining two homes, was too much for each of them to bear. Like Barry and Sandra, they respected each other as parents.

"We relate to each other as neighbors," Sonya said. As John echoed that statement he added, "And over the years we have become good neighbors. We've accepted our limitations. We just can't be the couple we thought we would always be when we got married. But so far it's working for us, and I doubt whether our children know that our lifestyle is any different than those of the parents of their friends."

For John and Sonya, there is clearly an emotional separation; but they have been able to continue in a living arrangement that they describe as benefiting everyone involved.

Ken and Darlene met in college and became very close friends. Both are gay. Most of their love relationships have been with same-sex partners. In spite of being gay, each of them always had a strong desire to have children. In their late twenties, they decided to try to have a child together—and, if that was successful, to have a second. They agreed that if Darlene became pregnant, they would marry, live together, and maintain a suitable household where the children would live. They also agreed that each would allow the other to have whatever parallel relationships he or she wanted to have, as long as those relationships would in no way interfere with their family life.

Ken and Darlene recognized from the very beginning that unless they made a commitment to their children—and decided that building a normal family environment would be their top priority—that this lifestyle they were designing would not work. It is now almost eleven years into Ken and Darlene's marriage, and both of them agree that it is working fine. The children—now ten and eight—don't know about their parent's unusual arrangement at this point. And the couple is undecided when, if ever, they will tell the children. They are not even sure it will ever be necessary for the children to know the unconventional nature of their parents' lifestyle.

These three cases describe situations where staying together for the children has been a choice that has worked. However, it is to be noted that they all have one very crucial element in common: There is an agreement between both partners about the motive and the necessity for the arrangement that they have made. In addition, each couple has managed to shield the children from the issues, dilemmas, and conflicts that their living arrangements have and probably will continue to raise.

CRITERIA FOR AND AGAINST HAVING A RELATIONSHIP "FOR THE CHILDREN"

Psychotherapists I have talked to differ sharply regarding this question. Some therapists routinely talk couples out of staying together solely for the children. After all, many studies have shown that children who grow up in "unhappy" intact homes fare far worst with respect to self-esteem and other measurable traits than do children who are raised in "happy" or less tense single-parent or stepparent homes. Yet other studies show that children of divorce show a more predictable series of negative psychological effects throughout their lifetime (and most typically in late childhood and early adolescence) than do children from intact homes.

An *unhappy* home—regardless of whether it is an intact, stepparent, or single-parent home—will normally provide a poor model of family life. Living in this atmosphere will probably have a negative impact on the self-esteem of any child. Children should therefore be protected from whatever tension is going on between their parents. If splitting up is the only way this can be accomplished, then a couple who is in the throes of divorce anyway will probably do little benefit to their children by staying together, if that means prolonging a negative climate.

In my experience, it might make sense to stay together for the children if:

• You can coexist without creating an air of constant anger and tension between you.

• You can change your expectations of each other in ways similar to what some of the couples illustrated earlier in this chapter have done.

• You can recognize the elements of your relationship that create tension. For example, if a nonsexual relationship with your partner is the only one that can comfortably exist between you, you make that part of your agreement, and unless there is a major change in each of your attitudes, you stick to it.

• You believe that it is most important to have the two parents together for the sake of the children. *But don't expect the children to thank you!* In other words, if this becomes a choice you make, recognize that at times it may be a source of unhappiness (even ultimately so). But, this is not your children's fault, and children should never be blamed for that choice or, under any circumstances, have it thrown into their faces. During a family therapy session in my office, one fourteen-year-old listened as his father said, "The only reason I stay with your mother is because of you." "Don't do me any favors, Dad!" he replied. It is a shame that the father did not have his son's wisdom.

• You and your partner can allow each other to lead separate lives (if that's what it takes). In addition, you will need to accept the implications of leading lives that are separate: This could mean you agree that certain things (such as outside relationships, people you date, or other activities that your partner is not involved with) just will not be discussed.

• You can remember that the environment in which the children will grow up has infinitely more of an impact on them than it will on you. If constant negative factors are present, they could affect your developing child forever.

In the criteria above, the assumption is that the couple would not be staying together except for the fact that there are children, and yet they agree to stay together. However, no matter how attractive the concept of keeping your family intact may be, there are times when it appears impossible. It is probably not advisable to stay together.

• If, after trying, it becomes apparent that no matter what you do, or how hard you try, you and your partner simply cannot lead a peaceful coexistence where there is a sufficient degree of happiness in your home.

• If there is another specific lifestyle that you would rather be following, and you find that you resent your children because of your inability or unwillingness to make the life change you are craving. This may be apparent if either you, your partner, or both of you find yourselves displacing anger onto your children because of your own feelings of unhappiness.

• If either parent abuses drugs or alcohol, or is abusive to the children or the other partner. Experience has shown that you can make every agreement under the sun, but all bets are off the minute abusive behavior kicks in. As we saw earlier in the book, *abusers don't change until they truly want to change, regardless of what they tell you when they are not being abusive.*

• If you are staying for any reason other than by choice. Some people stay in a relationship because they feel guilty about leaving or because they defer to a partner's threats. ("If you leave, you won't ever see the children"; "You won't get any money for support"; "I'll find someone else who *will* make a good parent, and replace you.") Remember, at the very least, the word *choice* implies that you have the freedom to go in either direction.

The choices that you and your partner make about staying together for the children are based on your own values and the level of cooperation that exists between the two of you. Remember, you are still a couple; Remember, too, that rule of thumb that says, Rarely does a lifestyle work for either of you that doesn't work for both of you.

OTHER REASONS COUPLES USE TO JUSTIFY STAYING TOGETHER

Over the years, I have seen many couples who would initially describe their relationship as being so bad or so empty that, within the first few minutes of the first session, I would find myself asking what would ever make them stay together under such circumstances. The answer couples most commonly give to that question is, "I don't know"—yet, they are together, and they stay together.

Other couples adopt a *celibate relationship*, where sex has simply stopped being an activity that they engage in together. There are couples in celibate marriages who love each other deeply, but lack a need for, or interest in, a sexual relationship. And since both partners feel this way, sexuality does not become a relationship issue. Of course, there can be many negative reasons for celibate marriages too, such as inhibited sexual desire, boredom, anger, and depression, such as I discussed in chapters 3 and 6.

You and your partner may be together for reasons other than sharing a satisfactory degree of passion and comfort:

• *Financial necessity.* Many couples feel trapped and unable to leave a relationship that is not working because of an inability to lead on their own the kind of lifestyle that they are accustomed to living as a couple. If this is the case, it could be your choice not to change your lifestyle to one you could afford on your own, so you stay. For some couples, their finances are so intertwined that the idea of going their separate ways becomes an overwhelming thought that is not entertained for long.

• *Religious beliefs and values that prohibit divorce.* In addition, many who don't believe in divorce are unwilling to separate without the option of remarriage.

• *A comfortable home environment* that you have established often makes it easy for you and your partner to avoid conflict simply by being immersed in other activities. If this is the case, then maybe to leave is to upset the apple cart in a way that would not be worth the benefits that you perceive you would gain by leaving.

• *Social reasons* have been known to keep many couples together. It is possible that you have a vast and meaningful social network that you might be excluded from if you and your partner were divorced or no longer together. Indeed, many couples relate best when they are in the presence of certain friends or their community of social contacts.

• *Status.* Throughout the ages, a common reason for couples who are dissatisfied with each other to continue to stay together has been to maintain their status. Along with this goes the shame that they perceive a separation or divorce would bring upon them. Many politicians, religious, and business leaders, who have used the image of an ideal home and family life as a part of the aura that propelled them to a prestigious position, do not want to jeopardize that image.

Your reasons for staying together need only one test: that the benefits of staying together outweigh the vast array of other alternatives available to you. Although the situations I have described above may not appear to be ideal, they have all worked for some couples. I remind you once again not to be fooled by the images of happiness you sometimes think tell the whole story about others you may even envy. Quite often, someone's wish is described as their reality; and the result of believing the image will be a disappointment when that image is measured against your less-than-ideal situation.

IF YOU DECIDE TO STAY

How long will a relationship last if it needs to be justified by the presence of children or the other factors we discussed? The infinite number of variables that go into a relationship make it impossible to predict. Indeed, many couples see themselves staying together, for whatever reasons, *one day at a time.* It is not uncommon to learn acceptance and to find yourselves slowly upgrading your relationship to where you start loving each other, even after you've written this possibility off. In addition, it is a choice that can be reevaluated constantly, and at any time. I only caution you not to let constant reevaluation of your commitment become more painful to you than any of the alternatives. Also, keep the following points in mind:

• It's worth repeating: *If you are staying together for the children, never blame them or vent your frustrations about what you are doing "for them" in front of them.* Even after the nastiest blowup, you may recover in a matter of moments; but your children could walk around with the residue of this negativity indefinitely. And, just as important, don't ever expect them to say "thank you."

• A hostile environment provides the worst possible role model for your children. With few exceptions, any of the alternative environments you could provide will probably be better for the children than that.

• Despite what other people may say, the children are often enough of a reason to stay together—or least they may compel you to try harder to work on the issues that have allowed your relationship to get to the point where considering these options is necessary.

• On the other hand, only you can decide if this is worth it—if the children or one of the other reasons you may have used to justify your relationship are truly reasons to stay together. What in fact do you have without those justifiable reasons? Is there a chance that your relationship can survive the children growing up? Is there at least the potential for a friendship between you and your partner?

Staying together for the children has become somewhat of a cliché. However, sometimes it is also used as an excuse to mask your own insecurities in going it alone for a while. If this is the case, in our next chapter we will talk about the issues of leaving a relationship, when, for one reason or another, that becomes the reality.

CHAPTER THIRTEEN

WHEN YOUR RELATIONSHIP HAS RUN ITS COURSE:

How to Get Out with Dignity

Getting over an ended love relationship is a skill that practically everyone will have to use at least once. For well over a decade, we've had a divorce rate of about 50 percent. Some studies have shown it to be somewhat higher, while others have produced slightly lower rates. I have not seen or heard of a credible study that hasn't put it within 10 percent of that 50 percent figure, which means that on average, half of those people who marry will have their relationships end in divorce. Add to that, ended relationships—live-in or otherwise—where the partners were not married and those who become widowed, and it's apparent that we are talking about something almost as common as relationships themselves.

The high divorce rate was not a function of the "me generation," as it was first thought to be. Sometime during the 1970s, it became a mainstream option to end a marriage that for whatever reason was not working. Many began to refer to the

divorce rates as "something that has reached epidemic proportions." Since the term "epidemic" is generally used in ref-
erence to disease, I would ask whether it is a worse condition
to find yourself exiting a situation that brings you more unhappiness than pleasure, or staying in a relationship that is
characterized by chronic unfulfillment.

Until recently, getting out of a marriage normally required
there to be one partner who was at fault and another who was
the innocent party, or the victim. With the proliferation of "no
fault divorce" (which in some form exists in just about every
state), the law has evolved more than some of our attitudes.

This chapter is for:

• Those of you who have been convinced for one reason or
another that your relationship must end.

• Those of you whose relationship has ended, not by your
choice but at the behest of your partner.

• Those who are trying to empathize with someone else who
is ending a relationship.

• Those trying to gain some insight into what they may have
gone through at other points in their lives.

• Those who wish they could leave but somehow see that
as being way "too hard," or who so fear going it alone that
they will put up with anything in order to avoid another bout
with single life.

It is this latter group—those who would like to leave but
who don't feel confident that they could pull it off—for whom
I coined the term "single phobia" in the lectures and talks that
I have given since my last book, *The Art of Living Single*, came
out. I believe that if there could ever be a widespread "cure"
for single phobia, the divorce rate would skyrocket even more—
I can't even predict how high. No trend can continue indefinitely, and this one will probably start swinging in the other
direction as soon as there becomes more of a tendency to choose
our partners more consciously. Then all it will take to slash
that divorce rate will be more attention to our relationship is-

sues, as well as more of a commitment to work them out together.

Becoming involved has traditionally been a function of the heart; but relationships that last do so with a lot of help from the head as well. We can't always choose who it is we will develop passionate feelings for, but we can work to make those feelings dissipate when having them toward someone is not in our best interest.

CAN IT BE CIVILIZED?

Yes, some couples are able to see that their relationship is no longer serving them, and agree to get out in style—that is, to make their breakup and divorce a civilized transition.

This is most possible in the following situations:

• There are no children involved, or if there are, there is a clear agreement as to what role each parent will play with respect to custody and visitation.

• You have come to a mutual decision; therefore no one is seen as the leaver or leavee, "winner" or "loser."

• There is no third party who is jealous of whatever relationship you have with the partner you are leaving (especially where there are children).

• You've been able to discuss intelligently those issues that may have triggered any of the negative emotions that made you turn to the option of breaking up in the first place.

• There is little passion left, or at least there is not one partner who is more romantically involved than the other.

As you can see by the above criteria, it is possible to work together as a couple to achieve this end if each of you is willing and sees the necessity to do so. This is especially important if there are children involved. That's why so many couples enter therapy together in order to make this transition as easy as possible.

WHEN YOU'RE THE ONE WHO HAS DECIDED TO LEAVE

If you're the one initiating the breakup, you can be in just as much pain as your partner, who may be seen by many as a "victim." In addition, you could be feeling an extraordinary amount of guilt toward your partner, your children, and others who are displeased by your decision. Likewise, many who initiate the breakup find themselves tormented by the tendency to second guess themselves, even if they have put as much consideration into this crucial decision as it deserves.

During lonely times or when you see your ex-partner in another light, it is easy to wonder whether you have made a mistake. What many find helpful is to write out a list of the reasons that helped you arrive at the decision to leave and to refer to that list often, but especially at those times when you find yourself doing that second guessing. This simple exercise has saved many from thoughtless reconciliations that not only don't last but tend to prolong the overall pain.

Telling a person that it's over is never easy either. Some find that the crutch that helps them the most through this painful task is their own rage, which will temporarily blind you to your feelings of guilt and confusion. It is usually more difficult to work this out with your partner in a calm and rational manner, but if you can manage to pull that off, you will probably be a lot more convincing. I asked several people whose partners had confronted them with the fact that their relationship was at an end what statement most convinced them that their partner was to be taken seriously? Some replies:

• "We no longer have enough between us to warrant the continuing of our relationship."
• "We have tried everything and we can't seem to change together, and I am not willing to go on trying and failing any longer."
• "I am not going to trust again that you will stop drinking. I want to leave even if you do."

- "I no longer love you."
- "I would rather die than spend another day with you. I want a divorce!"
- "I love you as a friend, but I have no more desire for you in any other way."
- "—— and I have agreed that as soon as I divorce you we will marry, so it's over."
- "I wish I could trade places with you and be the one who feels the pain, but I don't see how we can continue."

As you can see, some (but certainly not all) who initiate the breakup care deeply for their partners on some level. Many even initiate this process in a therapist's office, as a way of ensuring that their partners will have support to see them through.

WHEN YOUR PARTNER HAS INITIATED THE BREAKUP

Indeed, much of your pain here can result from feelings of helplessness and inadequacy. This might even be the case if you'd been thinking of initiating the breakup yourself, or if you fully agree with your partner that the relationship is no longer working.

Just as your partner, the initiator, has his or her feelings of guilt and confusion to contend with, you might be feeling undesirable. Conversely, you might have feelings of "renewed desire" for your partner, who now is no longer available. As strong as these feelings may get, they could be the expression of your panic or your addiction—either to your partner or to the lifestyle. Watch for a tendency to begin bargaining to get your partner back. In doing so, you may write off any other option of picking up the pieces of your life. The feeling that you can regain your partner is normally an illusion, since, chances are, it is not your former partner you want back, but some idealized version of him or her. After all, it is your partner as he or she really is who has initiated this breakup!

The remainder of this chapter will focus on helping you to free yourself, since in this case your only other option is to be saddled with what could be excruciating pain.

When letting go of an ended relationship—regardless of the circumstances—it is realistic to expect that there will be some emotional crisis. It doesn't matter who initiated the breakup; many of the issues are identical. This goes for those of you who have been widowed as well.

Since 1974, when I began writing about divorce and separation, I have seen a five-stage theory, an eight-stage theory, a seven-stage theory, and at least two six-stage theories. Fortunately, at some point I stopped counting, because letting go really boils down to two very major stages:

• *Becoming emotionally free of the relationship you have ended to the point where it no longer preoccupies you.* This includes putting all the emotions into perspective, handling the practical issues of this transition period, and seeing yourself—perhaps for the first time in decades—as someone who is not a part of a couple but an independent entity with a world full of options.

• *Rebuilding your life.* Once you have let go of the past, you are able to freely choose what you want your life to be now. It's important that these choices not be made as a reaction to your ended relationship, nor to merely quell the pain that you feel. Now you have the wisdom of experience on your side, and you can truly become the designer of your new life, limited only, perhaps, by external resources.

It is very difficult to go to that second stage and rebuild your life before you have truly let go. Many try to sidestep letting go and wind up in rebound relationships or other variations of "jumping out of the frying pan into the fire."

Of course, there are many who seem quite capable of leaving a relationship with little in the way of issues to work on, but, chances are, the relationship they are leaving was emotionally dead a long time before the formal ending took place.

THE ISSUES OF ENDING LOVE RELATIONSHIPS

There are basically two kinds of issues that people face when ending love relationships:

• *Practical issues.* Examples here include finance; learning and replacing certain skills and tasks that your former mate provided; child-rearing and visitation issues; legal issues; finding a new place to live; leaving your home and possibly beginning some new career options that may be necessary as a result of the breakup.

• *Emotional issues.* These are the feelings that are attributable to the breakup, divorce, or separation. They include loneliness, anger, depression, jealousy, fear, longing, grief, fear of the future, guilt (related to your ex-partner or children), resisting urges to contact your former partner, and dealing with the general stresses of transition.

In addition, there are some issues that come under both categories, such as dealing with your partners, family, and friends over the issues *they* may actually have about your breakup. This is a period in your life when it is most crucial to get support from those around you. Family and friends may be able to provide this to a limited degree. Many find support groups designed for those in transition to be extremely helpful in addition to support from professionals. These could include:

• *An attorney* who can help you assess your situation legally so that you are protected from things you may not even be presently anticipating, such as the hiding of marital property and records, protection of your children, and other interests depending on your situation. If you have recently broken up or are seriously anticipating doing so, it is never too early to consult an attorney who is qualified in handling the intricacies of divorce in your state. By arranging this consultation, you are not committing yourself to anything (other than the initial consultation fee); but you will probably find that the peace of mind is well worth it. Consulting an attorney does not mean that you are irrevocably moving toward divorce. It means only that you are getting information and perspective on your situation that can save you much agony later on.

Feel free to shop around for the type of attorney you can afford and one with whom you feel comfortable. Avoid attorneys who try to convince you to be angrier than you are or to go against your former partner in a way that you consider to be unfair. If, on the other hand, your partner has consulted this kind of "gladiator," you may have to find a suitable counterpart to protect your interests. These make the messiest divorces and, ironically, it is unusual that anyone comes out more a winner than the attorneys. But some people find it necessary to act out their anger toward their ex by applying legal torture.

• *Psychotherapy.* There is rarely a better use for group or individual psychotherapy than to help you to free yourself emotionally from an ended love relationship. The best form of therapy in this case is short-term goal-directed (behavioral or cognitive behavioral), which assumes that the intense feelings of rage, depression, and anxiety that you may be experiencing are adjustment reactions to the crisis you may now be undergoing.

Some therapists who meet a person at this time in his or her life make the mistake of diagnosing the depression and anxiety as something that has been there for a long time, and thus arrive at the conclusion that long-term therapy is the treatment of choice. Be aware of this when choosing a therapist, and to echo the advice that I gave about choosing lawyers, don't be afraid to seek a second opinion if you experience any discomfort with the therapist you've selected and his or her orientation for treatment with this issue.

Later in the chapter I will have more to say about getting support to help you through the transition, for it is this support that can provide you with the power tool you need to break free.

EMOTIONAL ROADBLOCKS TO BECOMING FREE

There are both practical and emotional issues in ending a love relationship, and since they often all come up at once, the mix can seem quite overwhelming. Practical issues, though rarely *easy*, are often *simple* to resolve, but they don't always feel simple because the emotional issues often can cast doubt around decisions you make. The reason I refer to them as simple is because of an observation I have made over many years of conducting divorce and separation groups. I am always struck by how efficiently one group member can advise another group member on how to handle his or her practical issues, and yet have so much difficulty with his or her own. The answer is obviously that in advising someone else, you are not emotionally vested. Therefore, by getting a handle on the emotional issues, I think you will find the practical ones will generally fall into place. But the first step is to sort them out.

For example, if it is necessary for you to move your place of residence, a practical solution would be to look into the types of houses or apartments you can afford, choose one, set a date for moving, and call a mover, etc. If, however, you are putting this task off after you have determined it is inevitable that it must be done, then perhaps you are doing so out of the emotional issue of anger connected with the fact that you have to move. This can apply to financial matters, job hunting, or any step that needs to be taken as part of the transition. So let's get right to the emotional issues that are standing in your way.

FIRST THE GOOD NEWS

The good news is that those emotions you are feeling are only temporary—although you may recognize that they sure don't feel that way! One of the most difficult things to do is to convince someone who is depressed over something as clear cut as ending a love relationship that the emotions they are feeling will go away. No mood is permanent. This is the essence of emotions—the good ones as well as the bad ones. They are transient in nature. And that goes for self-pity, guilt, bitterness, and feelings of loneliness, inadequacy, anger, mistrust, grief, desperation, and hopelessness.

When negative feelings linger, it is usually because of our self-defeating attitudes or irrational beliefs that keep them in place. To the extent that you have these irrational beliefs, it is to your benefit to look at what you may be telling yourself about the breakup, your former lifestyle, your partner, yourself, your children, or other people in your life who may have been in some way affected. This could be a part of the mix that is perpetuating the negative emotions you feel.

To the extent that you can adopt the alternative attitude (which is a rational belief), you will see a drastic reduction in the intensity of the feelings you may be experiencing.

ATTITUDES THAT PERPETUATE PAINFUL FEELINGS

• "I need him/her (or another ideal relationship) right now." Another version: "I must have a good mate to make me feel happy."

> *Associated Painful Feelings:* panic, loneliness, depression, desperation, craving, and anxiety.
> *Alternative Attitude* "I would prefer (as does practically every other person) a good relationship, but I do not *need* it right now in order to be at peace with myself. Furthermore, completely ideal relationships rarely exist."

• "Taking charge of my life without a partner is *too hard*," and, furthermore, "I shouldn't have to put up with these hassles at my age."

> *Associated Painful Feelings:* discomfort, anxiety, (low frustration tolerance).

Alternative Attitude "While I acknowledge that this is a very difficult time for me, calling it "too hard" is inaccurate because that implies impossible.

• "It's impossible to go through this period without feeling extremely depressed, angry, lonely, or jealous. Everyone says it's perfectly normal to feel this way."

Associated Feelings: helplessness, depression, anger, loneliness, and jealousy.

Alternative Attitude "While it is expected for me to feel *somewhat* depressed, angry, lonely, or jealous, it is not inevitable for me to feel horribly upset. Let me admit that I am creating these extreme feelings through my irrational beliefs. I can choose *not* to feel so upset by keeping levelheaded and refusing to blow things out of proportion."

• "After all I did for him/her all of these years, he/she *owes* me a lifetime of happiness" or, "I deserve better!"

Associated Feelings: self-righteous anger.

Alternative Attitude "While I truly gave a great deal in the relationship and would prefer to have lived happily ever after, I realize that giving a lot does not guarantee anything."

• "He or she *should/must* change his/her tune, treat me better, or at least be fair."

Associated Feelings: anger.

Alternative Attitude "It is unlikely that my mate will change his (or her) behavior toward me merely because I *want* him/her to do so. Changes that a person makes 'for' another person generally are not only temporary but packed with ulterior motives. True change comes because of one's *own* desire to change. So, by working on my own anger, it is possible, but hardly necessary, that my mate's attitude will change. Therefore I had better give up my demands and get on with my own life."

- "I have failed" or, "I am a failure."

  Associated Feelings: shame, guilt, and depression.
  Alternative Attitude "In reality, my relationship ran its course. That hardly makes *me* a failure. Believing I am a failure will only serve to make me depressed."

- "All men/women are alike."

  Associated Feelings: hopelessness (about getting involved again) and generalized anger.
  Alternative Attitude "I cannot accurately generalize the psychological traits of one man or woman to the traits of others. By overgeneralizing the traits of one person, and saying these traits apply to all members of the same sex, I will sabotage my becoming involved in a new relationship that might be more appropriate than the one which I am ending."

- "There will *never* be another like him/her."

  Associated Feelings: depression, grief, and panic.
  Alternative Attitude "There are many other fish in the sea."

- "I have ruined *everyone's* (including our children's) life by leaving, and I am a horrible person for doing so and for acting so selfishly."

  Associated Feelings: guilt.
  Alternative Attitude "Yes, it will be hard for others (such as our children) who depended on us being together. However, I believe I acted responsibly by leaving even though others will suffer from time to time. I will not put myself down because my actions contributed to others' discomfort.

- "I made the wrong choice! Now I have really ruined my life."

  Associated Feelings: depression, hopelessness, and jealousy.

Alternative Attitude "Well, I may have chosen wrongly, but at the time I chose my partner, I was acting on the facts and desires I had then. Too bad! Since foresight is rarely better than hindsight, it's now time to stop my own self-downing for my poor choice and get on with my life."

• "I am terrified of a future without my former mate. What will become of me!"

Associated Feelings: panic, hopelessness, and depression.
Alternative Attitude "I am not sure what will become of me, but I don't *have* to be sure. If I think of other situations where I felt like I was a fish out of water, I recall that I was able to adjust. I will adjust to this one too—as long as I do not convince myself that it is *too* hard, and that I can't adjust."

• "Others will reject me if I carry the 'stigma' of divorce. I will lose my family and friends, and that will be awful."

Associated Feelings: panic, depression, and shame.
Alternative Attitude "Yes, it is possible that some people will judge me harshly and perhaps be nasty and rejecting, but hopefully people whom I value the most will eventually accept what has happened as an unfortunate reality. Some may never accept it, and that will be disappointing, but since I am powerless to change *their* thinking, I'd better refuse to agree with them and refuse to put myself down. After all, whose life is it anyway?"

As you can see, the attitudes that cause you painful feelings—to the extent that you have them—will prevent you from letting go, while the alternative attitudes act to free you emotionally. Identify the attitudes you may be having that are keeping you from moving on. You may find it helpful to write the alternatives down on a three-by-five index card, carry it around with you, and refer to it several times a day when you start having twinges of the emotions that are brought on by those irrational beliefs. Learning the alternative attitudes has helped many people, and will certainly help you through this period.

ASKING FOR THE SUPPORT YOU NEED

Support is often the vehicle that makes the crucial difference in getting you through that process of letting go. While you may find it beneficial to get professional support, at a time like this many find it quite natural to turn to their family and friends. For some, that's all that is needed. For others, family and friends provide a great deal of the support that is needed, but not enough. Still others find that family and friends make poor sources of support. Perhaps the people who care about you are even more troubled by your breakup than you are, so they begin taking sides—or in some other way they put their own values into the forefront—when all you've really asked of them is to be there for you. Therefore, when seeking support to help you become emotionally free of an ended relationship, consider these points:

• You may find that the best form of support is a well-run *peer* support group. In such a group, you will be interacting with others who are going through the same transition you are. Contrary to what many believe, such support groups are not the "blind leading the blind." Instead, you will meet people who are handling—superbly—that very issue you are having the most difficulty with.

At the same time, you may find that you can often be a tremendous source of help for someone else with different issues. In addition, you may be ending a relationship at a point in your life when you are most open to meeting new friends. During the seventies, I was personally involved in starting many peer support groups. Some of them are still going on. Of course they are no longer divorce or separation groups, as those issues are long behind those who participated in the groups.

Instead, they become groups of friends that have stayed in touch.

It is to be anticipated that you will begin to experience those intense negative feelings such as anger, loneliness, and other cravings for your ex-partner. Make an arrangement with someone you can call upon if you simply need to talk at those moments. The availability of that type of support when you need it will make the cravings seem much more bearable. Eventually, you will experience them less and less.

• When you are receiving support, or giving someone else support, keep in mind that true support puts the goals of the person who is being supported in the forefront. If someone tries to overpower you with their values while you are in need of support, then they are not really being supportive to you at that moment.

• *Don't confuse sympathy with empathy.* Sympathy (except perhaps during those acute phases of a shock reaction to the most dire of circumstances) is often countersupportive. *When sympathizing with you, one usually validates your right to feel bad.* Empathy, on the other hand, provides a recognition of what you are feeling, but the emphasis is placed on helping you to move beyond that point.

• *Don't abuse your sources of support by maintaining a constantly one-sided relationship based solely on your needs, or by refusing to help yourself.* Many inadvertently push some of their best friends away. Remember, if you lean too hard, you can overpower whomever it is you are leaning on.

MATTERS OF TIME

Another aspect of ending a love relationship is that you get a gift of time. For some, this is an invaluable opportunity to do things with your life that have been up to now out of your reach. For others, this poses a problem in that you have a lot of time to kill. Use that time productively, to make plans, to do things you enjoy, to take care of other matters that need to be attended to. If you have found some suitable sources of support, trust that you gradually will begin to feel better and better—so put things into your life that you can look forward to.

- *First week.* This may be the week you most need to grieve. In addition, you have a number of practical issues to take care of. Fortunately, for many people, crisis makes them very efficient in taking care of these things. Get whatever you need for yourself to get through it, but be aware of that tendency to become overpowered by your emotions.
- *Second week.* The shock has probably subsided, but this is the week when many report that their cravings for the former "idealized" mate or lifestyle are most acute. Perhaps you will be all right for a while and then feelings of rage, depression, grief, loneliness, or desperation will hit you. If you can use your support system properly, after this week you may have been through the worst of it.
- *Third week.* Most people report that cravings are beginning to lessen now, although when they do occur, they will probably be just as intense as in week two. But the fact that they may be coming less frequently should help you to feel as though you are on your way.
- *Fourth week.* There are still cravings, but in terms of pure intensity, the worst is probably over. If this is not the case, and you have not yet done so, this could be the time to seek professional help.

The next several months—usually up to the end of the first year—are experienced differently by different people. For some, these months are an emotional roller coaster, whereas for others, there is a leveling off as permanent healing begins to occur. My favorite guideline regarding when it is finally prudent for most people to think about getting reinvolved in another long-term relationship is about a year, but more on that later.

DEALING WITH YOUR EX

If you have been the initiator, it is likely that your ex is quite angry at you. People who have been in some of the most emotionally abusive relationships have told me that what went on after the separation made what went on in the marriage tame by comparison. If this is the case, it is extremely important that you maintain whatever distance is necessary to prevent whatever consequences—emotional or physical—that could result. This is especially important when there are children around who under the best of circumstances would find your breakup difficult, but for whom emotional abuse at this point could be devastating. Therefore, if this is the situation and there is any way that you can set things up so that you and your ex don't have to see each other, a lot of hassle can be prevented.

An ex-partner who is intentionally trying to make things difficult for you may need to be dealt with by legal means. These include obtaining a restraining order and/or supervised visitation that is court-mandated. If necessary, this can be arranged through your attorney.

However, what is possibly even more difficult to handle are the longings that you may experience when you see your ex. Unfortunately, there is no legal solution for this. Many couples who split up with an array of unresolved feelings are able to become friends once they are no longer involved emotionally. However, during a period of emotional firestorm, avoidance is the best technique. If you decide to reconcile (and I'll have more to say about that in the next chapter), that decision needs to be well thought out. Chances are, many issues that wreaked havoc when you were together will need to be resolved first. In my experience, spontaneous reconciliations, based on a spark of passion that could be rekindled when you least expect it, usually don't last.

DEALING WITH CHILDREN AFTER DIVORCE

There are many excellent books on this subject, both directed at children and at parents, such as those written by Richard Garner, M.D. And although doing this topic complete justice is beyond the scope of this book, please be aware of these major points:

• *Your ex will always be your child's parent.* Never put your ex down in front of the children. Parents who do this typically succeed only in turning their children against themselves. If both parents do it, the product is an extremely confused child. Your children will continue to form their own opinions of both their parents, but attempting to poison a child's mind (and the younger he or she is, the more this applies) is a form of child abuse.

• *Help your children to acknowledge the reality of your divorce,* but never let them believe that they are to blame. To children, there is no such thing as a no-fault divorce. Often the result is their tendency to blame themselves. This results in their own lack of self-esteem, as well as almost every other form of emotional distress, which can lead to behavior problems, drug and alcohol abuse, and chronic feelings of inadequacy and mistrust.

• *Don't give your child false hope that you will get back together.* Except under the most extreme circumstances, one rarely meets a child who would not like to see his or her home intact. But false hopes don't help either.

• *Help them return to their familiar routines as quickly as possible, while resolving their feelings of loss.* Constantly reinforce the idea that neither parent has divorced *them.* And unless there is some special reason why this is not advisable, encourage as positive a relationship as possible with your ex to develop—especially if you are the custodial parent.

Children do recover from their parents' divorce, if their needs are attended to. As difficult as it may be when you are feeling your own grief, remember that you will recover more easily than they will. The best thing you can give your child is your own example as a person who enjoys life and who is emotionally equipped to ultimately enjoy meaningful relationships.

BREAKING UP IS HARD TO DO— BUT NOT IMPOSSIBLE

• "I would get over this in no time if only my ex would move far away."

• "In reality, I was lonelier when we were together than I could ever be now that we are apart."

• "We were actually married quite happily for five years, but it's a shame that our marriage lasted eighteen."

• "Life alone is simpler, quieter, and more manageable, but the price to pay is loneliness."

• "It took almost a year for me to realize that the world doesn't have a meeting every morning at eight o'clock to decide how to make my life miserable."

• "For about six months, I would have loved to have gotten my hands on whoever it was that said 'It is better to have loved and lost than not to have loved at all,' but slowly that cliché is starting to make sense."

I could easily fill three books this size quoting people who have expressed their feelings about their breakups. Indeed, getting through this is a process that is similar for many people, but there are always unique elements that you have to be aware of. So, use some of these additional points to help you in your own healing process:

• *Remember that* simple *and* easy *are not synonymous.* As simple as it may seem to break away, expecting that it will be easy is a sure route to disappointment. Expect that you will have doubts and bouts of second-guessing yourself, and you may even have occasional relapses when you'll feel as though you broke up yesterday. If you don't take these relapses too seriously, they won't become major obstacles.

• *No matter how deeply you felt for your ex-partner, those feelings belong to you.* Don't delude yourself into believing that you can't have them again for someone else. (If that were the case, who could ever blame you for not letting go?)

• *Try doing a postmortem on your relationship without blaming either your partner or yourself.* Understand what worked and what didn't work. What can you learn from this experience that can benefit you the next time around? What would you do differently if you had it to do over again? If you can tap this self-knowledge as a resource, you are in possession of a gold mine of information about yourself.

• *If the relationship you are ending was a short-term one, remember that not everything works out.* On the other hand if it was long-term, try to focus on what you had together as an invaluable life experience; few life experiences are all good or all bad. Think about it. Someone who has broken up with you—who does not really care about you—has done you a favor in the long run. You are now free to pursue the rest of your life.

• *If the ending of your relationship makes you feel like a victim, be aware of whether this characterizes other things in your life as well.* For example, if your relationship hadn't ended, might you be just as likely to be saying when you are eighty years old, "I gave it all up for my marriage"?

• *Forgiving your ex is to your advantage.* A lot has been romanticized about the concept of forgiveness. In addition, practically all religions deal with the actual act of forgiving as a positive virtue, but what isn't stressed enough is the fact that once you have truly forgiven, you relieve yourself of a great deal of anger, anxiety, frustration, and tension. This also means that you have taken another major step toward freeing yourself so that you can move on emotionally. Forgiving does not mean condoning or admitting that you were wrong. Forgiving simply means letting go of the negative emotions that you experience toward a person and adopting more or less of a "live and let live" attitude of acceptance. Until this is done on some level, the healing process will not be complete.

• *If you are having feelings of inadequacy, try some new things.* Take risks. You may need to learn some skills that you depended on your ex for. All these things may be possible now with the time that you now have as a by-product of your new freedom. It can be an exhilarating feeling to take a risk when things turn out well, but you win even when they don't. In that case, taking the risk teaches you that you are not as fragile as you may have thought you were.

• *Learn to enjoy your own solitude and aloneness as an alternative to the loneliness you may initially feel.* Remember, your own solitude can be extremely nourishing, and it is one thing that nobody can ever take away from you.

• Those who heal the quickest are those who never—even for a moment—lose hope that their lives will continue to get better. You will help the process by understanding that the responsibility for making it better lies firmly with yourself!

TOWARD YOUR NEXT RELATIONSHIP

There are two common errors that are made when it comes to entering a new relationship after a breakup:

• *Closing yourself off to all members of the opposite sex*—by telling yourself that, after all you have been through, you are not going to be hurt again, or that there is no such thing as a good partner. This attitude is common with those who have not dealt with their anger and who continue to blame their ex for what may have been a painful relationship and/or breakup. If you fear your own vulnerabilities so much that you will avoid new relationships altogether, remember the "worst" has already happened to you, and you *did* live through it. If you tell yourself you could never go through that experience again, you may close the door to an important life experience. Hopefully you have learned something, and you will now proceed with a bit more caution. But demanding a guarantee that should you become involved again that you won't be hurt is a guarantee only that you will stay uninvolved.

• *Getting involved with the first (or the second, third, or fourth) person* you meet a very short time after you have split. In this case, it could be your fear of never getting involved again or of just plain going it alone that makes you the rebounder we've discussed in chapters 1 and 7. Make that next relationship a true choice by waiting until you've done all the healing you need to do. For most people, this takes about a year. As one very happily remated person told me recently: "I was ready about five minutes after I felt the joy of being free. I knew then that for someone to make me give this up, they would have to be quite special."

If you let only your heart decide last time, this time try letting your head in on the decision as well.

> ## THE CRISIS IS OVER, NOW WHAT?—TOWARD REBUILDING YOUR LIFE

When you have achieved a degree of emotional separateness from your relationship, you'll know it.

• If it has been your tendency to remember only the good times, you will start remembering the bad times as well. By the same token, don't have something akin to amnesia about remembering what brought the two of you together in the first place. Also, don't make more or less of it. When you are free, you will be much more able to see both sides of the coin.

• It is perfectionistic, as well as unrealistic, to expect that you will never have occasional relapses. These can take any form. If you can ignore them, or in some way distract yourself, they will probably pass. Some people are fine until they hear that their ex has remarried—maybe years later—and then they begin the whole process of second-guessing themselves again. Know that these feelings are normal and their impact will be minimal.

Most of all, getting out with dignity once your relationship has run its course involves your own ability to give yourself permission to pick up the pieces and go in any of life's infinite directions. That permission is perhaps the greatest gift you can give yourself.

CHAPTER FOURTEEN

RECHOOSING EACH OTHER

If there is one point that I have taken great pains to get across throughout this book, it is my belief that life is a series of choices that we make. Some choices are made with great zeal, while others are made by default. Thus, while I wrote this book to help you to find ways to keep your relationship together, I hope you will do so after considering the many alternatives that are available. Then you are truly choosing, and your relationship can become a vehicle for happiness and growth for both you and your partner.

In this chapter I will talk about some of the issues that couples who are reconciling after a breakup might consider. The balance of the chapter will be devoted to all of you whose choice at this moment is to move straight ahead with your present partner. This may include rekindling and planning (or replanning) your lives together. I will end with some further perspectives on staying together.

RECONCILIATION AFTER A BREAKUP

Many couples have told me over the years that their relationship didn't *really* start until after they had broken up—and, in many cases, had even divorced and stayed that way for several years—and then chosen to reconcile. If you've never had that experience, you might think of the breakup as an unnecessary step for a couple who is going to wind up together anyway. But as some who needed a total break and reconciliation before their relationships could really work will tell you, the process was anything but unfortunate:

• "We never realized what we had until it was gone. Then getting back together again was better than our initial courtship. We rarely get upset about petty things anymore since we have been back together."

• "Once he wasn't around and I could realize that I needed to take responsibility for my own unhappiness rather than blaming it on him, I could then for the first time really be open to a relationship."

• "As bad as I thought he was, I needed a real jolt to see that there was no one else that I came even close to valuing as much as I valued him."

• The husband of the woman who was quoted just above said, "I really never thought about my wife when we were together; I just took her for granted. But when she wasn't around, I realized what a quality person she really was."

• "Being divorced turned into a crash course on learning how to care for someone. If we hadn't gotten back together again, I'm sure I would have survived; but I will never let our marriage get out of hand again."

Of course, not everyone who reconciles talks about it in glowing terms:

• "I can't believe I put myself through the same hell of a painful breakup twice."

• "I would have never gone back if I weren't feeling desperate to be in a relationship. But going back did show me once and for all that it can't work."

• "I must have been crazy to think that it would be any different. Nothing changed. No issues were resolved. I jumped out of the fire and went right back into the same frying pan. When I left the second time, it wasn't nearly as painful."

When is it appropriate to reconcile? This is another one of those questions that is best answered by encouraging you to ask some questions of yourself:

• Do both you and your partner understand the mistakes that were made and the issues that were unresolved when you left? Do you both agree on the areas of your relationship that will need to be worked through so that you can prevent a relapse? Are both of you accepting your due share of the "blame"?

• Has the separation turned both of you around to the point where it has allowed you to mature in the areas that made you contribute to the breakup?

• Are you able to focus once again on the positive aspects of your partner? Is your desire to go back grounded mainly in desire for your partner?

• Can you remember the past you shared together without getting caught up in the bad times? Can you now forgive and, once and for all, let go of whatever anger and resentment you are harboring against your partner?

• Are you now willing to accept your partner for who he or she is, even though your partner still has the habits you didn't like the first time around? Can you let go of the nitpicking and try again with *no guarantee* that he or she has changed? If you or your partner has changed in a significant way, have the changes been ones you've chosen for yourself rather than to accommodate your partner so that you can reconcile?

• Are you now more willing to compromise? Are you willing to take the time to give this relationship and your partner the attention needed to work together toward providing fulfillment for each other?

To the extent that you can answer yes to these questions, you are making a good case for reconciliation. Below are some other questions that will examine the other side of the coin:

• Is your desire to go back primarily grounded in your discovery that the singles world is no bed of roses? Is it loneliness or any other form of desperation that you are mostly seeking to avoid? Are you preoccupied with preventing your partner from getting involved with someone else?
• Is your desire to go back based on guilt (concerning the children or your ex-partner)? Jealousy? Financial insecurity?

To the extent that you have answered yes to the questions above, there is an indication that the reconciliation will be short-lived. Partners who reconcile out of desire for each other and out of the realization that they wanted each other in the first place have the best chance of their reconciliation working. On the other hand, couples who use reconciliation as an anesthesia for the pain they are experiencing in connection with being out on their own are, in essence, entering rebound relationships. As we have seen earlier, rebound relationships usually don't have a good prognosis.

You know what your issues were. If there is a commitment, this time, to do whatever is necessary to deal with them—and also to deal with new issues that may have arisen due to the breakup itself—then you have truly rechosen each other. If it doesn't work out, then perhaps you will find in retrospect that reconciliation was the only way you could part without serious doubts. If you decide to reconcile and it doesn't work out, *chances are it will not be as painful the second time as it was the first.* In my experience, however, it is quite common for people to fear a second breakup much more than they feared the first one.

REKINDLING

When your relationship seems to have lost (or misplaced) its spark, and both you and your partner want to do whatever it takes to rekindle it, the question most often asked is whether that is possible. The answer is, sometimes. Look for the following things to be present when it can be rekindled:

- The right ingredients were there in the first place.
- Underneath the pain that has been straining the relationship, there is genuine caring and at least an acceptable amount of passion for each of you to build on.
- The desire toward rekindling is there on the part of both of you.
- There is a commitment to work on the issues that will bring this about.

If you are in this situation, I urge you to look back at Chapters 3 and 6.

Rekindling simply means giving a relationship that may have gone somewhat off course a push in the right direction. This is a form of rechoosing each other, since the alternative is often feelings that become more and more indifferent until that spark truly goes out. As we've seen earlier, there is a point at which it may be too late. But as long as you both feel a commitment to work toward rekindling, that point has not been reached.

PLANNING YOUR FUTURE TOGETHER

It has become commonplace for people to make one-, five-, ten- and twenty-year career goals. Many couples talk about the years ahead and find that setting their goals as a couple helps to reinforce their commitment to each other. In doing this, then, perhaps you and your partner can have some of the following discussions together:

• *What do you hope that your lives will be like this time next year?* In five years? In ten years? In fifteen years? In twenty years? What are your goals both individually and together as a couple? What would you like to see your lifestyle become? In what ways do you think you can use some growth? What obstacles do you hope to overcome?

• *Making vows.* Married couples think nothing of making lifetime vows, but our high divorce rate shows that those vows are often formalities imposed on them by religion or the law in order to marry, rather than something that they truly feel. What are your vows together as a couple? If you wrote them out (and many couples who marry today do), what would they be? Write them down. Refer to them from time to time when things inevitably start to go off course. Remember, they are *your* chosen vows, not someone else's.

• *In addition to having a discussion about your future, try visualizing your future.* Just what would be the story of your lives if that story worked out exactly the way you wanted it to? What is necessary to get there? What is within your power to help you get there? How much are you merely depending on luck, and how much are you depending on what is within your ability to achieve?

• *What do you hope that your later years will be like?* Some couples wait way too long to think about that—and find themselves disappointed with what is there. Are you likely to be someone who later on in life talks about all the things you should have done when you were the age you are now? Think back to how your life was five years ago. If you had it to do all over again, what would you have done differently? What do you envision your answer to that will be five years from now? Discuss this with your partner. Try to work with each other as a team to meet those crucial goals. One of the realizations of life is that there is no compensation for misfortune. So the more you can take responsibility to put your destiny within your own grip, the less you will blame yourself for what you don't have later on.

• *Think about that period of time when the children will be gone.* Perhaps that is a time when your relationship and career can be at its best. However, for many who become "empty nest-ers"—a time of life that so many look forward to—disappoint-ment, boredom, and regret are the results. Many have found that this became the most serious crisis of their relationship or their lives. If being a parent has been your main focus in life up to this point, what will replace it once your children—as healthy children do—begin their own lives? People who plan this properly are much more likely to find those years to be ones that were well worth waiting for. Those who didn't plan may greet the time when their children grow up with feelings of emptiness.

Planning your lives together not only helps you to address these crucial issues before they become sources of crisis, it also sends a message between partners that the future includes each other. What a way to make rechoosing each other an ongoing process!

TOWARD STAYING TOGETHER

As we have seen throughout this book, it takes much more than good fortune to make a relationship work. Here are some final perspectives that you can put to work for you:

• *Keep current with your issues and feelings.* Much of what I have seen over the years that has made a potentially solid long-term relationship fall apart has been things that could have been handled at the appropriate time with unbelievable ease.
• *Consciously make the effort to spend time together.* Avoid hav-ing what amounts to a relationship-in-passing. By now, hope-fully, you have learned the importance of valuing each other and making each other a priority. Remember, drifting apart is a quiet and slow process.
• *Feeling intense feelings of love and desire is one aspect of a re-lationship,* and so are negative feelings on the other side of the spectrum. But the best relationships are grounded in the qui-etness of day-to-day living. Avoid demanding only intensely

good times, for the result may be pressure, stress, and a tendency to look elsewhere.

• *Would you now rechoose your partner?* Ask that question of yourself often. Whenever you begin to think that you wouldn't, stop and look for the underlying issue. Some couples actually put it on their calendars to ask this question of themselves every so often. A business, no matter how profitable, will fall apart if it is not attended to. Relationships work the same way. As easy as it may seem to do at times, don't take yourselves for granted.

• *Few relationships can fulfill all of the needs of both partners.* When you start feeling unfulfilled, take a look and see if all your eggs are in one basket. The best couples are those who can stand on their own two feet, be independent, and yet be quite caring and connected at the same time. Give your partner the appropriate amount of space and privacy. I believe this is the essence of a mature relationship.

• *In the best relationships there is a commitment to openness and honesty.* But don't be so brutally honest that it becomes a source of hurt for your partner.

• *The happiest couples I have known are those whose partners encourage each other to pursue what is important to him or her.* Sometimes this involves helping your partner toward a certain goal, and at other times it involves letting him or her be.

• *Building trust is another one of those ongoing processes that I view as crucial.* Be aware of things that you may do to put a wedge between the two of you, such as airing issues (that are the exclusive property of the relationship) to family or friends. And just as important as keeping trust alive is keeping blame to a minimum. When I do couples therapy, what I see most frequently is each partner wanting confirmation that he or she is being correct and right while the other partner is at fault. As important as solving the presenting problem is, I find that helping the couple to break that habit of blaming to be far more important.

As I said early in this book, the things that attracted you to your partner and made you desire more involvement are not the same things that will keep you together. But I urge you to go back to that time and remember how you may have flirted with each other, gotten off on the lightness of the moment, made each other something special, and as a result really enjoyed not only your partner *but the person that* you *were when you were with your partner*. You may have changed some, but you are still the same people you were then, and much of what you had then can be incorporated into your day-to-day living, if only you make it a priority.

I hope you will consider the skills in this book as a set of tools to help you to change something in your relationship or to accept those things about your partner that can't be changed. Do either as frequently as the need arises. Go back through this book often as new issues emerge, or any time you wish for some perspective on an old issue. Rechoosing each other is a commitment to keep passion and comfort in your relationship. It is also a pledge to keep a special bond between you. Think of this ongoing process as one with ongoing rewards—both in the outcome and in sharing what it takes to get there.